How to Believe
In a Sagittarius

Real Life Guidance on How to
Get Along and be Friends with the 9th
Sign of the Zodiac

How to Believe
In a Sagittarius

Real Life Guidance on How to
Get Along and be Friends with the 9th
Sign of the Zodiac

Mary L. English

BOOKS

Winchester, UK
Washington, USA

First published by O-Books, 2012
O-Books is an imprint of John Hunt Publishing Ltd., Laurel House, Station Approach,
Alresford, Hants, SO24 9JH, UK
office1@o-books.net
www.o-books.com

For distributor details and how to order please visit the 'Ordering' section on our website.

Text copyright: Mary L. English 2011

ISBN: 978 1 84694 861 9

A CIP catalogue record for this book is available from the British Library.

Design: Stuart Davies

Printed in the UK by CPI Antony Rowe
Printed in the USA by Offset Paperback Mfrs, Inc

We operate a distinctive and ethical publishing philosophy in all
areas of our business, from our global network of authors to
production and worldwide distribution.

CONTENTS

Dedication

This book is dedicated to and in loving memory of my father:

Noel Francis Benedict Egerton English

22-12-1921 to 22-9-1982

May he rest in peace.

We are the clay; and
and Thou our potter;
and we all the
work of Thy hand.

Isaiah 64.8

Acknowledgements

I would like to thank the following people:

Clare McCulloch who helped change the title of this book with the word 'in',

My grateful thanks will always follow you and your dreams.

Mabel, Jessica and Usha for their Homeopathic help and understanding.

Laura and Mandy for their friendship.

Donna Cunningham for her generous help and advice.

Judy Hall for her wonderful Sagittarian inspiration.

Peter K for the motorbike trips.

Alois Treindl for being the Pisces that founded the wonderful Astro.com website.

Judy Ramsell Howard at the Bach Centre for her encouragement.

John my publisher for being the person that fought tooth and nail to get this book published and all the staff at O-Books including Stuart, Trevor, Kate, Catherine, Nick, Maria and Mary.

My editor Elizabeth Radley for her fine touch…

Oksana, Radcliff, Elizabeth, Lucy and Rose for their welcome editing eyes.

And last but not least my lovely clients for their valued contributions.

Introduction

"Sagittarius is the eternal traveller engaged in unceasing exploration of the physical and philosophical worlds... Its symbol is the centaur, half man, half beast, a synthesis of instinct and rational thought, capable of making a spontaneous, intuitional leap into the unknown which pulls ever onwards."[2]
Judy Hall

Why the title of this book?

I didn't set out to write twelve astrology books. I only started with one, which was about my own sign and entitled *How to Survive a Pisces*, to help the people living with Pisceans understand that particular sign. However, when I had written it and it was published, friends and clients asked me if I was going to write about *their* sign, and it was at that point that I realised I had got myself a rather lengthy project!

And since I had started with the last sign of the Zodiac, I thought it best that I should go backwards through all the signs. So I wrote *How to Bond with an Aquarius* and *How to Cheer Up a Capricorn*, and now here I am, with the ninth sign of the Zodiac, Sagittarius.

What made writing this book more personal was the fact that my dearly departed father was a Sagittarius, and a few of my friends are also the same sign. Knowing somebody well makes writing about their sign that much easier. There are pluses and minuses about writing about someone who has died, as it brings up lots of old memories. And since my dad died when I was only 22, a lot of time has passed since my experience of him, so please excuse me if my memory of him isn't the same as yours.

Strangely enough, while my dad was terminally ill, I became friends with another Sagittarius, who is still in my life now... even if he'd rather not be! That's not to say that this particular person replaced my dad, but he certainly filled an astrological gap in my life.

He also has no belief in astrology.

His only comment on the subject once was, after saying how ridiculous the whole thing is:

"Well, at least you make a living doing it!"

And there we have a typical Sagittarius comment. Something to the point, no floweriness, no subtlety, just saying it as it is. He's quite right. I do make a living from astrology but not as much as I did in my retailing career. In reality I made far more money moving boxes of socks for C & A than I have ever done in my present career. However, I now have far more fun, which completely outweighs the financial limitations.

So what is it about Sagittarius that feels the need to say things as they are? To point out the bleeding obvious? To take your breath away with seemingly rude or at least unsubtle observations?

My dad came out with a great one once. Our Leo cousin was visiting, and as Dad was greeting her at the front door, he happened to let slip: "You're looking very fat!" This was a bit choice as my father was overweight himself and it really *isn't* the sort of thing you say to a Leo.

It wasn't untrue, she had put on a bit of weight, but did he really need to point that out? It must have played havoc with his Libra Moon, which always makes such a point of being polite. However, even though my cousin was a little thrown by this comment, the visit carried on in a perfectly amenable manner and no one got into a strop. I don't know how he did it, but he did, and I expect the person concerned has completely forgotten this episode and I will tell you why.

Sagittarius is such a delightful, upbeat, infectious, fun-loving energy that you can't help but be excited about what they are currently being excited about. Ruled by benevolent Jupiter king of the gods, who we shall learn about a minute, Sagittarius wants to take you to a place of wonder, a place where you will say: "Wow!"

And it is that 'wow' that we're going to learn about in this book.

Before we can understand Sagittarius we need to learn a little bit about Astrology, where it came from and where it is today.

Astrology is the science that explores the action of celestial bodies upon animate and inanimate objects, and their reactions to such influences.[1]

Astrology dates back to early human civilization and is the parent of astronomy; for many years they were one science. Modern astrology has its source in what was called Sumer and is now known as Iraq.

The people there, who called their land Sumer, quite suddenly and inexplicably began to build large, walled cities out of sun-dried mud bricks on the banks of the two great rivers (Tigris and Euphrates)... In time, the growing wealth of the cities led to the formation of a non-productive priestly class, who had both the opportunity and the incentive to study the stars. These men were the first astrologers.[1]

Christopher McIntosh, a historian, tell us in his *The Astrologers and Their Creed*:

The priests of this kingdom made the discovery, which developed into what we now call astronomy and the zodiacal system of the planets, which we call astrology today. For many generations they painstakingly recorded the movements of these heavenly bodies. Eventually, they discovered, by careful calculation, that in addition to the Sun and the Moon, five other visible planets moved in specific directions every day. These were the planets that we now call Mercury, Venus, Mars, Jupiter and Saturn.

The priests lived highly secluded lives in monasteries adjacent to massive pyramidal observation towers called ziqqurats. Every day they observed the movements of the planets and noted down any corresponding earthly phenomena from floods to rebellions. They came to the conclusion that the laws which governed the movements of the stars and planets also governed events on Earth.

In the beginning the stars and planets were regarded as being actual gods. Later, as religion became more sophisticated, the two ideas were separated and the belief developed that the god 'ruled' the corresponding planet.

Gradually, a highly complex system was built up in which each planet had a particular set of properties ascribed to it. This system was developed partly through the reports of the priests and partly though the natural characteristics of the planets. Mars was seen to be red in colour and was therefore identified with the god Nergal, the fiery god of war and destruction.

Venus, identified by the Sumerians as their goddess Inanna, was the most prominent in the morning, giving birth, as it were, to the day. She therefore became the planet associated with the female qualities of love, gentleness and reproduction.

The observation of the stars by the Sumerians was mostly a religious act. The planets were their gods and each visible object was associated with an invisible spiritual being that judged their actions, blessed them with good fortune or sent them tribulations.

A slight case of projection, but none the less, the movement of the planets helped the Sumerians develop some meaning and make sense of their lives as they had got the hang of farming and land management, and the more mundane aspects of life. Having got the practical issues of life under control they now wanted to explore their spiritual selves. Astrology and the study of the planets allowed them to do this.

These Sumerian priests made associations between earthly events like floods and famine with a particular phase of the Moon, by seeing an evening 'star' or by the appearance of a comet. After a time they then noted that these 'heavenly bodies' had various cycles and it became possible for them to mathematically determine when, for instance, the Moon might be eclipsed, so they could then forecast certain events. This information was reserved only for the king and was not distributed on the mass scale as it is today.

Astrology didn't happen overnight. It began with observation, something that is somewhat lost in the modern world. We don't have the time today to watch, wait and observe. We read about something, see it on the telly, go out and buy it and expect 'bingo' for our problems to cease. Time for contemplation and observation is reserved for Tibetan monks or the clinically depressed.

In medieval times Astrologers were also Astronomers. They knew where the stars and the planets were, plus they were educated and could read and write. With the advent of schools and computers, we can now enjoy the fruits of these people's hard work by turning a page or clicking a mouse, but nothing will replace observing how people are and how they interact with each other.

And it is with this 'observing eye' we're going to learn about the 9th sign of the Zodiac, their beliefs and why believing *in* them is so important.

Mary L English
Bath 2011

Chapter I

The Sign

"Sagittarius needs time to ponder, space to assimilate and formulate a belief system which offers a way to Be. It must live out its beliefs by Being. A centaur paying lip-service to ethics is a hollow shell, purposeless and untrustworthy. A Sagittarius who is what it believes, is a sage who leads mankind onwards into knowledge of itself, its world and other dimensions of being."[3]
Sagittarius Judy Hall, *The Karmic Journey*

Sagittarius is the ninth sign of the Zodiac. To call someone a Sagittarius they have to be born between a certain set of dates when the Sun was in the sign of Sagittarius. When we say 'in the sign' what we actually mean is, the Sun (literally) is in the part of the sky above that we call Sagittarius. Astrology isn't complicated, once you grasp the basic ideas, one of which is we divide the sky into 12 equal parts, which start at the Aries point in the Spring. This bit of the sky, which is calculated astronomically, is the beginning of the Zodiac.

The ancient Babylonians worked out their bits of the sky using the constellations of stars, but since that was hundreds of year ago, the planets have shifted in their orbit and the constellations now don't match-up with the sky divisions.

Don't worry!

As far as we're concerned, the sky can still be divided up equally by using the first day of Spring as our starting point... and 9 segments on from there is our friend Sagittarius. The dates when this happens vary every year but mostly occur from November 22nd to December 21st.

We will be using an online resource, so you can get those

figures accurately but they're a rough guide for the moment. Sagittarius is ruled by a planet called Jupiter. Each zodiac star sign has a planet that looks after it, which we call its 'ruler'. This is a sort of categorizing of each sign and has only evolved because of the breadth of the English language. However, it'll make more sense when I explain a bit about Jupiter the planet itself.

King of the Planets

Unlike Uranus, Neptune and Pluto, Jupiter was never 'discovered' as even the Babylonians, the original instigators of astrology, could see it with the naked eye from Earth.

Astronomers call Jupiter "the undisputed king of the planets" as it is the first of the so-called gas giants.

It is so big and one of the brightest objects in the heavens. Jupiter twinkles by reflecting light from the Sun, however, it emits more than twice as much energy as it receives from the Sun and is one of the noisiest objects in the sky.

It also has a powerful magnetic field.

While writing this book Jupiter was very visible in the night sky in the sign of Pisces, and I spent a number of evenings photographing it when it lined up with the Moon. It's amazing to think that even though Jupiter is between 893 million and 964 million kilometres from the Earth, I can still see it in my back garden.

Now keeping in mind that the Earth itself is (at the equator) 12,756 kilometres wide (diameter), then Jupiter is over 70,006 times the width of the Earth away from us, and I can still see it. So imagine, then, that it must be pretty big!

Gas Giant

Jupiter is made of hydrogen and helium gas with some methane mixed in, so there is no solid surface to walk on like that of the Moon. These gases form beautiful horizontal stripes across its surface. It travels so fast it makes a complete rotation every ten hours so it makes you wonder if you'd grow older quicker living there!

Spinning around it are 63 satellites, four of which are called Moons and they can be seen through binoculars, and look like a little string of pearls.

Now, Astrology takes the description of a planet, mixes it with some keywords and 'bingo' produces its attributes.

So.

As Jupiter is a gas giant, we talk in Astrology about it magnifying and making bigger things that it connects with. Someone with Jupiter in their chart, near their Sun sign, will be one of those people given to 'overdoing' things or exaggerating.

We also use some of the stories from myths and legends (this is the bit I like) and add it to the mix. In the Greek myths Jupiter was called Zeus and Eve Jackson in: *Jupiter: An Astrologer's Guide* describes him like this:

Zeus is generally depicted as a man of middle years, bearded and imposing, wearing his aegis or goatskin of divine power and his cloak sometimes sky blue, sometimes the deep blue of the night sky, spangled with stars. Among his many titles are King, Saviour, Father, Descender, Kindly One, Friend, Giver of Completeness, God of Marriage, Protector of Strangers, Counsellor, Cloud-Gatherer, Thunderer, Protector of Oaths.

So here we have 'someone' who is a fatherly figure, friendly, kind and philosophical... but also, when he's had a bad day, capable of throwing his thunderbolts and scaring the natives.

When the Babylonians originally viewed Jupiter, they called him Marduk: the son of the Sun God. In the myths of the time, he organised the chaos of the universe, created the constellations, decided the boundary lines of the fixed year and also:

Set up three stars for each of the 12 months.[4]

Quite a busy chap!

As Astrology travelled across the world from east to west via Greece, and developed and changed as it went, Jupiter became what he is today, the Great Benefactor. There to guide us and help us on our life journey, our spiritual path.

Now, I don't want you getting the idea that ALL Sagittarians worship a god or follow a belief system. That's not entirely true. Not every member of your local congregation will be a Sagittarius, and not every Bible Basher is one too. I do know Sagittarians who would never even think of religion, but they do tend to have what I call a religious substitute, like computers, or sport; something they *treat* like religion but isn't thought of as that way.

My dad was a Sagittarius, and a very devout Catholic. His parents and grandparents and all the way back to our family coming to England from Ireland were all Catholics and he wouldn't have it any other way. He loved his religion and I never heard him question it in any way.

I didn't share his enthusiasm. To my mind Catholics (especially the nuns who taught me) were all bonkers, some more than others. I just couldn't see his religion his way, and became a Pagan, which I still am today.

But the other Sagittarians I know treat football or computers like their religion and woe betide you if you criticize their pet theories or stuff-they-have-worked-out-themselves. That's a definite 'No-No'.

So I thought I'd ask a Sagittarius for a few key points about their psyche.

Here we have Mandi, a Homeopath and occasional actor. She was born and lives in New York City and is married with two sons. She 'survived' Catholic school and is politically active and has always had an interest in alternative medicine.

I asked her: What is your definition of belief?

"If you can picture it in your mind or feel it in your bones, it exists."

What was the first time you had to believe something (as opposed to know it/experience it... i.e. Father Christmas) and what happened to that belief, do you still believe it now?

"My dog died when I was 5. The nun told me when I was seven that he didn't have an immortal soul and was not waiting for me in heaven. All I could think of was how stupid this woman was and I just knew he was waiting for me in heaven. And I still believe that now – that every-thing that exists has a life-force and exists in some form forever."

What is your religious/spiritual persuasion?

"Best I can define it is: Born-Again Pagan. Or maybe Weekend Wicca."

What religion (if any) are your parents?

"Catholic"

On a scale of % (100% being the biggest) how optimistic about your life are you?

"95% – It's very difficult for me not to see the potential in every-thing."

What makes you cross?

"When people are purposefully mean. I can't abide meanness. And people telling me what I can and can't do. Never tell me I can't do something."

What makes you happy?

"My kids. A really good piece of Theatre. A good meal with good friends. Seeing new places and things. And a good yell-out-loud orgasm."

Notice the lack of subtlety. Notice how she describes herself and the words she uses. They are to-the-point with no frivolous bits. She states it as it is, in an upbeat, positive way. There's no grudges there. The nuns were wrong, she was right... end of!

Astrological Descriptions

Before we can truly describe a Sagittarius, we have to consider how astrologers have described them in the past. Is our Sagittarius the same person today?

Let's ask Herbert T Waite author of *The New Waite's Compendium of Natal Astrology* (originally written in 1917, rewritten in 1953 by Colin Evans, and brought-up-to-date in 1967 by Brian Gardener) what he thinks about Sagittarians:

Sagittarius individuals are optimistic, cheerful, honourable, loyal, independent, enterprising and very active. They possess a natural gift for prophecy and wonderful intuition. The higher class of Sagittarian combines a keen sense of justice with a philosophical, innately religious, kind and merciful nature. People seem to gravitate to them for guidance in both spiritual and material matters... Finding their greatest pleasure in life in showing others that All is Law, and that all the pain and discord are due to the fact that this great truth has yet to be internally realised by the majority of mankind... at his worst, the plausible toady and hypocrite, chiefly in the domains of the Church, the law, and politics, since these constitute his natural bent.

Hmm, quite a flattering portrayal for the 'higher class'... not so flattering for 'the worst'...

Let's see what Linda Goodman said in 1968 in her *Linda Goodman's Sun Signs*:

What it is on the archer's mind and heart is almost instantly on his lips. He's as frank and earnest as a six year old. You can take that old advice, 'If you want the truth, go to a child,' and switch it to 'If you want the truth, go to a Sagittarian.'... Few people can resent the archer for very long, because he is so transparently free of harmful intent. You'll see this lovable, likeable, intelligent idealist almost anywhere or any time... It's a rare Sagittarian who doesn't have a matched set of luggage. They love to travel, and there's usually at least one suitcase, well worn from hundreds of trips, that's kept packed and ready for instant use.

Getting more of a picture now.

Let's check with what Marion D March and Joan McEvers said in 1976 in *The Only Way to Learn Astrology Volume 1*:

straight forward, philosophical, freedom loving, broadminded, optimistic, enthusiastic, talkative, self-indulgent, blunt, pushy.

There seems to be a thread running through this.

Let's ask Felix Lyle and see what he thought in 1998 in his *The Instant Astrologer*:

As this sign's symbol, the half-human, half-horse centaur suggests, Sagittarius has a distinctly dual nature. One half represents reason – the higher mind probing the universe, searching for meaning – while the other symbolizes instinctual passion. This latter side of Sagittarius simply wants to 'horse around', occasionally in a thoroughly dissolute and licentious manner. The big dilemma for this spirited, changeable sign, therefore, is whether it is ruled by the head of a man or the rear end of a horse.

Crikey, I hadn't thought about the horse element. Is this true?

And lastly let's ask Rae Orion in her wonderfully useful book from 1999 *Astrology for Dummies*:

Independent, honest, and filled with a sense of possibility, you feel most alive when you are having an adventure in the world.

I think we can safely say after reading these descriptions that the four major keywords that describe Sagittarius are: adventurous, philosophical, independent... and tactless.

Adventurous

To understand a Sagittarius, you need to first of all understand their main motivation. On a very basic level, they love to travel, the further the better. My father spent months away from the family home, travelling the world as a sales manager for a large pharmaceutical company. He never seemed to tire of packing or unpacking a suitcase. He loved to talk about the places he had visited, the food that he had eaten and where he had explored. Every city had a story, which he would tell with enthusiasm and excitement. As he was multilingual and enjoyed the challenge of new languages, he could feel 'at home' wherever he went.

Matthew lives in Massachusetts, USA, and has a degree in mathematics and works in computer software. Here he tells us a little about why he loves/loved travel so much:

I always felt that the act of travelling gave me perspective on my life. I used to love it. Now I'm more of a stay-at-home because air travel is just too much of a pain with security etc. The attitude is partially compounded by years of business travel.

I then asked him what was it about travel that he liked so much?

Long car rides for vacations. The difference in the feeling of different places. Then a few air travel vacations – same effect. Then national and international business travel and exposure to different cultures. The effects of not speaking the local language, but managing to get by – heightened awareness to compensate for the language issue. Different food. Etc.

It's the differences that he loves. The getting on an aeroplane and going to somewhere that he hasn't been to before.

Just to hear both sides of the story, I then asked a young lady about her experience of travel.

Louise is a professional astrologer and lives in New Mexico,

USA. She has Scorpio Ascendant, and has Sun and Moon in Sagittarius:

I have always loved travel. As a kid I was fascinated by airports. Still am! The idea of just getting on a plane and going somewhere completely new. For a Sagittarius I think it's about freedom, not being restricted, also enjoying exploring different cultures, etc. Now I do more metaphysical travel, which I also love. The same Sagittarian themes of freedom and exploration apply.

So for Louise, it's the "going somewhere completely new." Both she and Matthew love the different cultures and the sense of excitement about that 'newness'.

Marie is a Life Coach and lives in LA California with her son. She has Sagittarius Ascendant. She has a lot to say about her love of travel:

First of all, I love seeing the variety of topography, colors, rocks, plants, and forms the earth has to offer. I can really grasp the infinite of the universe and the insignificance of my life in the grand scheme of things when I'm looking at billion year old rock formations in southern Utah and contemplate the events, heat, moisture, weather, and geological phenomena that occurred to produce the magnificent colors, striations and curls in the rocks... let alone the epochs that have transpired and the fossils and infinite mysteries that lay buried in the rocks all over the planet. I find this alone extraordinary. Time seems so incomprehensible to me when I'm traveling in some places where you can conceive of the magnitude of life.

Notice how she uses the words "magnitude of life." For her, life isn't teeny and quiet...

I have learned more about my faith, perspective, humanity, life, and God the more I've travelled. I've felt more connected with my creator standing on the edge of the Grand Canyon than in a church. The sense of leaving what is familiar is a path towards experiencing faith. Especially if you are as inclined as I am to traverse the US without a map and or a planned itinerary, which I've done quite a bit. A drive is vital to me. The longer the better. I need to escape to get new perspectives, to get me out of my limited thinking about my life. I honestly get buggy if I do not travel once every couple of months. Some days I need to see how far I can drive in any direction just to get out of my head or an energy circuit. I have driven cross-country, and from Chicago to California taking a different route every time, fascinated with the surprises of life. I love surprises, which is why I enjoy travel, as well. And few places fail to offer me something I didn't expect, pleasant or not.

So for Marie, travel helps stop her having a limited view of her life, helps her 'get out of her head' and helps her feel more connected 'with the creator'.

This is strong stuff. Travelling for her is not just a pootle along the motorway to a service station lunch, or a little meander to the countryside to have a cuppa with some friends. Travel adds *meaning* to her life.

I then asked Steve who is 48 and works in an advertising agency in Brisbane, Australia what his views on travel are. He is a Sagittarius with Moon in Libra:

Travel to me now is not such a big deal as it once was. If I think back to the first time I went overseas it was a real adventure. It wasn't just a trip, it was to go live in another country although I went with two new friends whom I met through work, rather than through my normal friend network. One was transferring to a new position, the other was a surfing friend of his who wanted to experience new horizons. I had spent a year seeking work in a recession and another 18 months with my nose to the grindstone. I wanted change. I made the decision to join them in an instant and a month or so later took off.

Boarding that plane was like opening a book, or starting a new chapter. That's how I viewed travel then, with the excitement and anticipation of beginning a new chapter in my life. Like embarking on another, completely different more expansive lifestyle, with new experiences; in some respects I was a new person too as I was free to be myself unencumbered with peer group pressures or expectations, no limiting history or baggage other than what I carried myself, which wasn't much. Who knew what opportunities tomorrow held?

Sitting in that plane at take-off was the most wonderful, exciting feeling of anticipation and freedom. It wasn't just a book I was reading, I was living it.

For Steve, then, travel to somewhere new was giving him the opportunity to live a new life, start fresh, make a new person of himself, 'a real adventure'. He also felt "free to be myself" which we will cover when we get to independent...

Philosophical

My Oxford dictionary of current English defines philosophy as: "The use of reason and argument in search for truth and knowledge of reality, especially of the causes and nature of things, and the principles governing existence, perception, human behaviour, and the material universe." It also defines philosophical as "skilled in or devoted to philosophy."

William Blake the English poet, a Sagittarian with a sensitive Cancer Ascendant and Cancer Moon, must have come out with one of the most-quoted philosophical sayings in his poem *Auguries of Innocence*:

To see a World in Grain of Sand
And Heaven in a Wild Flower
Hold Infinity in the palm of your hand
And Eternity in an hour

He goes on to describe how wounding, misusing, killing, being jealous of, poisoning and mocking sentient beings and those caught up in poverty "deform the human race." In my mind you can't get more philosophical than that.

That's not to say that Sagittarians are philosophers themselves, in an official, professional capacity (they tend to be Taurus or Aries) but they do have the capacity to summarise in a succinct way, something we might find confusing. It's that 'tell it as it is' capacity that is so typical.

When I was halfway through writing this book, as it is a book about Sagittarius and philosophical wisdom, I thought I would study an AS-level in philosophy, mistakenly thinking that I would discover a number of philosophers who were this sign. This was not the case. The subject is now an academic procedure and, even though extremely interesting, is more about being able to argue your point and less about the wonders of life.

However, you can guarantee that your average and not so average Sagittarius will have their own 'life philosophy' and sprinkled throughout Chapters 3, 4 and 5 are little quotes from various Sagittarians about their view of life.

Noel Coward, a wonderfully funny Sagittarian entertainer with Libra Ascendant (polite) and Moon in Gemini (chatty), when asked in 1949 what his life philosophy was replied:

My philosophy is as simple as ever. I love smoking, drinking, moderate sexual intercourse on a diminishing scale, reading and writing (not arithmetic). I have a selfless absorption in the well-being and achievements of Noël Coward... In spite of my unregenerate spiritual attitude, I am jolly kind to everybody and still attentive and devoted to my dear old Mother.

Another description of philosophy is its original Greek meaning as 'love of wisdom'. Because, that's the point, Sagittarians love wisdom and the pursuit of wisdom, whatever that might be today.

One person I find so inspiring musically is Ludovico Einaudi, the Italian composer. He has an Aquarius Ascendant, Sun in the 10th and Moon in squishy Pisces. (I know this because I asked him his birth time when I saw him in Bristol.)

Here he is talking to Tony Watts about his album *Nightbook*:

I had the idea of the night as a place where all the thoughts you don't have time to open up in the day, they are there to be explored. Different doors of experience. And music takes you through those doors to get in touch with them within an infinite zone.

All my music is a voyage," he explains. *"Music that helps you journey into yourself – to listen to what is in there. The answers to our questions that are there waiting to be heard if we block out the hubbub of everyday and tune ourselves in.*

Independent

"Although I'm independent I love male company, I want a companion who wants to be my equal, not dominate me or wither under me."
Sagittarius female on a dating website

Unlike an Aquarius who needs to feel mentally free to think about weird and wacky things, Sagittarius sense of freedom is gained through their love of long-distance travel and learning about other cultures. Their love of freedom can result in them not being in *any* rush to get married until or unless they find a partner who can either enjoy the travelling with them, or will allow them to do it on their own.

My Oxford dictionary of current English defines independent as: *"not depending on authority or control; self-governing; not depending on another thing for validity etc, or on another person for one's opinion or livelihood; unwilling to be under obligation to others."*

These short phrases beautifully sum up our friends the Sagittarius' attitudes to independence. They definitely do *not* like being told what to do, so consequently will spend a lot of time telling *others* what they should be doing.

If you think about some of the famous Sagittarians such as Frank Sinatra, Beethoven, Edith Piaf, Britney Spears, Walt Disney, Noel Coward, Woody Allen, Tina Turner, Winston Churchill and Bruce Lee the image that would come to mind would be of someone who is their own boss and is delivering the orders, rather than receiving them! Their independence is not unfriendly or unwelcoming, it's just a deep desire to have the freedom to do their own thing.

When Sagittarian Jane Fonda, Capricorn Ascendant (responsible/serious), Moon in Leo (likes to shine) was asked about her feminist views in her book *My Life So Far* she mentioned why she'd actually written it:

One of the reasons that I wrote the book is because I wanted to show that you don't have to be dependent on a man financially – you can be famous and successful and financially independent – and still have these feelings that if I'm not with a man, I don't really exist... I approached my work from a feminist perspective, and I read the books – but in my body, in the center of me, I couldn't be an embodied feminist. Because somewhere I knew that if I did, my husband would not stay with me [laughs] and of course he didn't.[5]

So here she was struggling with her feminist views, which didn't reconcile with her being married. Now, I'm sure it's perfectly possible to be married and be a feminist but the issue here was also about having financial freedom. In her case the dilemma was with her Sagittarius Sun, and her Capricorn Ascendant. One part of her wanted to 'behave', the other wanted to 'do her own thing' and be free.

My dad took quite a while to 'settle down'. When he was 22

he was posted to India as he had joined the 5th Royal Gurkha Regiment during the Second World War and in those days, people wrote each other letters. No mobiles or computers then! My grandfather (Libra) and my grandmother (Capricorn) wrote regularly to him. In April 1943 my grandfather wrote a short note at the end of my grandmother's letter:

I am just adding a line to Mother's to wish you every happiness on your decision to link your life with Maureen. We do not know her but I have complete faith in your judgement and feel certain you have done wisely. If you and she are of the same mind when this B war is over I hope you will get fixed up soon and spend many, many happy years together.

Dad had obviously got engaged to someone while he was out there (I have no idea where she was living)… but the engagement didn't last long…

Four months later my grandfather wrote again, this time the letter is slightly less warm, in fact he tells my dad off for not writing sooner and for also not writing to his intended!

Dear Noel, I am hoping you will be so surprised at receiving this letter from me that you will be stung into writing to us as it is ages since we had word from you… Maureen also said in her last letter that she had not heard from you for a long time and seemed rather hurt about it. If you intend to keep your engagement to her you should write fairly frequently and also to your Mother.

As it was, the engagement broke off and it was another eight years or so before my dad finally settled down and married my mother.

My mother is an Aquarius and she and my dad got on very well. I never heard them argue about anything. But then my dad was away for months of the year, and even when he retired, he died soon after, so maybe they would have disagreed about a few things when they were older, we'll never know. What I do know is that when my dad was retired early from his job, he set up his own company. There was no thought of working for someone else, he had the contacts and off he went, selling English pottery abroad.

Tactless

"Like many Sags, a lot of these more annoying characteristics are somehow forgivable. I'm quite convinced that only a Sag can say and do the things they do and still manage to get away with it."
Aries wife of a Sagittarian Businessman

I often wonder where Sagittarius tactlessness comes from and does it really exist? I suppose it's evolved because to feel passionate about something, and to want to spend your time 'finding the truth' in the world, then you're also going to have to be honest and with honesty sometimes comes hurtful truth.

The sort of truths we'd rather avoid.

A bit like the story of Emperor's New Clothes where the swindler weavers make the Emperor a new suit from invisible material, but they tell the Emperor that only the wise can see the cloth, and those that are stupid can't see it. So, of course the Emperor doesn't want to be perceived as stupid, and goes along with the process. But it's the child who witnesses the procession who pipes up with: "The Emperor is naked!" in the way that children do, and the Emperor has to then deal with where his pride and vanity have taken him.

To those in the crowd, the child at first is perceived as being cheeky or causing a fuss, but when everyone around him realises 'the truth' they then believe the child's version of events.

So, to call a Sagittarius tactless, we must be talking about pride, vanity, self-importance and superiority, things that a

Sagittarius (generally) doesn't suffer from.

To have the truth, certain behaviours will have to go by the board and be ignored.

As I mentioned in the introduction, my father was the epitome of politeness and well-brought-up-ness (as he had Moon in Libra) and knew how to use his knife and fork and what sort of things to say to priests, vicars and ladies, but when someone came into view (our cousin) who was bigger than he remembered, he just *had* to point it out. And it wasn't a judgment; it was a statement of fact.

Cousin = Bigger = Fact = Truth

Here is a lovely account from a young lady who lives in the Baltic States in Northern Europe:

My uncle (my mother's brother, a Cancer) is married to a Sagittarius. She's impossible not to notice. When she is in the room everyone will know that she is here, what's her name, where she's from, and that she is STILL here... She likes to be in the centre of attention and is not shy to say it aloud. My grandfather used to work as a diplomat, so he knows a lot of "important" people, and attends many official functions. And those important people come to his birthday parties... And if my uncle and his wife also attend (they live in another country, so they are not around all the time), there will be a scandal the next day about her behaviour, that it's inappropriate, that she doesn't understand how to behave, that she should at least 'act normal' among such people, and everything like that... And I was always told how she is such a bad example...

So her Auntie (I love Aunties, see my book How to Bond with an Aquarius!) obviously doesn't have the necessary social skills or respect or reverence for these what I call 'posh people' ...

But she also has some great qualities. She is a very honest person. Behind that kind of behaviour hides complete openness and honesty and even sensitivity. When I get to talk to her one-on-one, not in public, she's like a completely different person. A very good listener, very understanding and very wise. When I was a teenager I trusted her more than my own mother, talked to her a lot about everything I never dared to talk about with my mother, and she gave me some very good advice I am still grateful for. Because of her loudness and activeness others think she can't keep a secret, but that's not true. I know she kept a lot of mine. I love her for her honesty and for being someone I can completely trust.

Milayo is Sagittarius (who we will learn more about in Chapter 8) and her Aquarius son Nkera (who we met in How to Bond with an Aquarius) tells us a little about his mother's bluntness:

She can be blunt almost to the point of tactlessness and if someone else has an idea she doesn't like, she will quickly tell them so, suggest alternatives and then promptly switch off if they try to persist (very annoying) or just get bewildered (if she's losing an argument she believes in).

And here we have it. Even though a Sagittarius might make you want to squirm with embarrassment at their lack of deportment or current fashionable niceties, underneath is someone wanting Complete Truth and Honesty.

Chapter 2

How to Make a Chart

For the newbie making a birth chart can seem a daunting prospect. Not any longer. There are plenty of websites and plenty of books, of which this is one, that can gently guide you in making a chart and more importantly making sense of the information in it.

Most people I know don't want to spend money on something they don't understand so we're going to use a website that has free online resources. This particular website is Swiss, so you can be assured the information will be precise and reliable. The secret is to provide the correct information, so the birth chart you produce is accurate.

There are three pieces of important information that we need first before we can make a birth chart.

We need the date of birth, the place of birth and the time of birth.

The general dates for someone to be called a Sagittarius are 22nd November to 21st December.

As astrology is based on the movement of the planets, and the planets are moving all the time, an accurate birth time is important.

Let's say, if your friend/relative was born at 5.30 AM in the morning in London, England, on the 22nd November 1985 they'd be a Scorpio, but if they were born in the same location but at 2.30PM in the afternoon, they'd be our friend the Sagittarius as the Sun was changing sign on that day.

So an accurate birth time is very important...

AAA = Accuracy Aids Adaptation

Now, I'd just like to dispel myth here. There is no such thing as a cusp. You are either one sign or another.

Yes, there is a dividing line, but the planets are calculated with each sign containing 30° so that with the 12 signs all added up together we get 360° which is the total amount of degrees in a circle.

Your Sagittarius might be 0° 4 mins Sagittarius, or 29° 58 mins Sagittarius, but they are still a Sagittarius. There is a huge difference between the signs. Scorpio, Sagittarius and Capricorn are so different, let's not muddle them up!

So, go to www.astro.com, make an account, then go to the website page called 'Free Horoscopes', and look down the page at the section called 'Extended Chart Selection'.

Click on this link

We're going to make your chart using a system called Equal House. This means each house or section of the birth chart is going to be equal in size. The default system on this website is called Placidus, which makes the house sizes all squiffy and unequal. I'm sure it is a very valuable system but it's not one that I use.

Enter all your data: date, time and location of birth in the top boxes. If you scroll down the page a teeny bit you will find the section called **Options**. It will say House System, and in that box you will see 'default'. Change the default to say equal and leave everything else as it is.

The lines in the centre of the chart are either easy or challenging mathematical associations between each planet in the chart, so ignore them too.

We only want three pieces of information. The **sign** of the **Ascendant**, the **sign** the **Moon** is in and the **house** the **Sun** is in.

This is the abbreviation for the Ascendant:

AC

This is the symbol for the Sun:

This is the symbol for the Moon:

The houses are numbered 1-12 in an anti-clockwise order.

These are the shapes representing the signs, so find the one that matches yours. They are called glyphs.

Aries ♈
Taurus ♉
Gemini ♊
Cancer ♋
Leo ♌
Virgo ♍
Libra ♎
Scorpio ♏
Sagittarius ♐
Capricorn ♑
Aquarius ♒
Pisces ♓

The Elements

To understand your Sagittarius fully, you must take into account the Element of their Ascendant and Moon. Each sign of the Zodiac has been given an Element that it operates under: Earth, Air, Fire and Water. I like to think of them as operating at different 'speeds'.

The **Earth** signs are **Taurus**, **Virgo** and **Capricorn**.

The Earth Element is stable, grounded and concerned with practical matters. A Sagittarius with a lot of Earth in their chart works best at a very slow, steady speed. I refer to these in the text as 'Earthy'.

The **Air** signs are **Gemini**, **Libra** and **Aquarius** (who is the 'Water-carrier' *not* a water sign). The Air Element enjoys ideas, concepts and thoughts. It operates at a faster speed than Earth, not as fast as Fire but faster than Water and Earth. Imagine them as being medium speed.

The **Fire** signs are **Aries**, **Leo** and our good friend **Sagittarius**. The Fire Element likes action, excitement and can be very impatient. Their speed is *very* fast. I refer to these as Firey i.e. Fire-Sign not Fiery as in quick-tempered.

The **Water** signs are **Cancer, Scorpio** and **Pisces**.

The Water Element involves feelings, impressions, hunches and intuition. They operate faster than Earth but not as fast as the air. A sort of slow-medium speed.

Chapter 3

The Ascendant

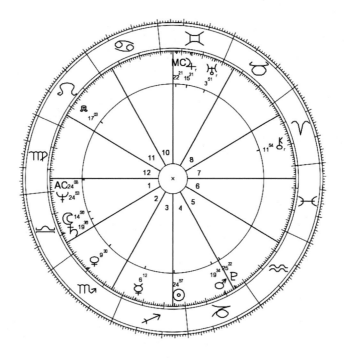

In our example, Jane Austen has a Virgo Ascendant. This made her good at paying attention to detail and a good communicator because Mercury the communication planet rules Virgo. As the author of over six novels, with Sense and Sensibility containing more than 123,000 words, a hefty achievement, she had the concentration necessary to hone her craft.

As Virgo is also the sign of health and healing it meant she would have been concerned with health;

Everybody's heart is open, you know, when they have recently escaped from severe pain, or are recovering the blessing of health.

She could also (on a bad day), be a dreadful worrier. Here's Jane writing to her (Capricorn) sister Cassandra on the 18th Dec 1798:

My Mother continues hearty, her appetite & nights are very good, but her Bowels are still not entirely settled, & she sometimes complains of an Asthma, a Dropsy, Water in her Chest & a Liver Disorder.[4]

Crikey! With that amount of things wrong with someone, you'd think they were at death's door – but Mrs Austen (her mother) lived until the ripe old age of 88, while Jane died aged only 41.

To find out an accurate Ascendant you need to find the exact time of birth as the rising sign changes every two hours. Once you've found out the correct Ascendant, you have now discovered the motivating factor for that person. As the Ascendant is determined by the exact moment of birth, it represents in astrology how we view life. You could use the words to describe this as the 'glasses' or the 'coat' you wear, or as our 'front door' to our world.

Astrology sees the Ascendant sign as being the one we are most likely to express when under stress or automatically. It's also the sign your family will see as the real you. Most other people in your life will only see your Ascendant sign and will tend to treat you accordingly. Getting an understanding of someone's Ascendant helps you understand them much better than just knowing their Sun sign.

Aries Ascendant

"My idea of superwoman is someone who scrubs her own floors."
Bette Midler, Sun in the 8th

As the first Fire sign of the Zodiac, and ruled by Mars the God of war, Aries the Ram wants to get things done ASAP. Not famed for their levels of patience and their likelihood to run over any subtle plans you might have, the courage of their convictions will keep you safe. If you want someone to move heaven and earth for you, Aries Ascendant fits the bill.

Taurus Ascendant

"Sometimes when you have everything, you can't really tell what matters."
Christina Onassis, Sun in the 7th

Taurus is an earth sign and a slow, steady energy. They want their world to be practical, earthy and financially stable. Ruled by Venus the Goddess of Love it's important to remember that sex, sensuality and their physical self are extremely important.

Gemini Ascendant

"The mind is a beautiful instrument if you know how to be a no-mind too."
Bhagwan Shree Ragneesh, Sun in the 7th

The airy Gemini energy is ideally placed to make for a good communicator. Ruled by Mercury the flighty god of communication, the ability to chat, twitter, mobile-update, Facebook is their *raison d'être*. Their life will be a constant flutter of change, new jobs, new home/s, and interesting new friendships.

Cancer Ascendant

"What is the price of experience? Do men buy it for a song? Or wisdom for a dance in the street? No, it is bought with the price of all the man hath, his house, his wife, his children."
William Blake, Sun in the 5th

The water sign Cancer concerns itself with nurturing and heightened emotions. Ruled by the Moon, our constant reflective light, Cancer Ascendant wants to ensure that everyone is safe and snugly. Moody, emotional, and loving all living beings, including abandoned puppies and/or fluffy kittens, having a family and loved-ones close is a high priority.

Leo Ascendant

"I need that on stage. I need a burst of life. That's entertainment for me."
Tina Turner Sun, in the 4th

Leo is a fire sign, and as King of the Jungle needs recognition, red carpets, and an adoring fan base. You're not going to miss this combination; they light up the room as they enter. Smiles and laughter are all that is needed as they are ruled by the Sun, the bringer of daylight and sunshine.

Virgo Ascendant

"I'm not one of those crazy people who wash constantly and put little white gloves on before I touch a doorknob or something. I'm not that crazy, but I do wash my hands for what I know to be a sufficient amount of time."
Woody Allen, Sun in the 4th

The Earth sign Virgo (ruled by our tricky little friend Mercury) enjoys dotting the i's and crossing the t's. If you're not careful, their long 'to-do' lists, worries and funny little foibles will totally take over your life. As Virgo is square to Sagittarius there is surely some inner conflict which will need to be resolved before they can feel content.

Libra Ascendant

"With love, you should go ahead and take the risk of getting hurt... because love is an amazing feeling."

Britney Spears, Sun in the 3rd

The air sign Libra is ruled by Venus our loving Goddess and wants everyone to get on and live happily ever after. Close personal relationships are a high priority, which is slightly at odds with Sagittarius' freedom-loving principles. Communes, open relationships and equal sharing of love and affection make for a complex outlook.

Scorpio Ascendant

"As far as I'm concerned, love means fighting, big fat lies, and a couple of slaps across the face."

Edith Piaf Sun, in the 2nd

The water sign Scorpio is an ace at emotional mind games. Ruled by Pluto the planet of power and transformation makes this Ascendant search for trust and loyalty. However the world is a notoriously unpredictable place, which can strike fear and cause no end of jealousy, distrust and suspicion.

Sagittarius Ascendant

"Music makes me high on stage, and that's the truth. It's like being almost addicted to music."

Jimi Hendrix,Sun in the 12th

Now we have a double helping of the Sagittarius mix. This Fire sign wants to shoot its metaphorical arrows as far into the sky as it can. Nothing can hold back inspiration and a sheer enjoyment of life and all its pleasures.

Capricorn Ascendant

"My mother killed herself when I was 12. I won't complete that relationship. But I can try to understand her."
Jane Fonda, Sun in the 12th

This Earth sign Ascendant makes for a serious, focused exterior. Ruled by stern Saturn, nothing will escape its critical opinion. Sensible solutions and realistic expectations are part of its joy. It can also withstand more setbacks than other sign combinations.

Aquarius Ascendant

"A friend is someone who gives you total freedom to be yourself."
Jim Morrisson, Sun in the 11th

Friendly Aquarius ruled by wacky Uranus gives a view on life that is truly original. Differentness and ideas are what motivate this Ascendant and needing to have friends to share that with.

Pisces Ascendant

"And you and I left with the same old question, the sheer unspeakable strangeness of being here at all."
Robin Williamson, Sun in the 9th

Sensitive, watery, emotional Pisces the fishes enables the Sagittarius vision to see things that others can only sense. With such a watery Ascendant, it makes our Sagittarius a little more able to empathise, a little more absorbed in the wonders of creation and more wanting to have 'meaning' in their life.

Chapter 4

The Moon

If the Sun rules our ego and self-expression, the Moon reflects and absorbs our inner emotional self just like it does in 'real life' with the Moon reflecting the light of the Sun and representing how we feel. It also represents our inner child. The part of us that is young, playful and in need of nurturing. Truly understanding our Moon sign and allowing it to feel that nurturing makes for a much happier life.

Problems arise when the Moon and the Sun are at odds with each other. Say your Sagittarius has Moon in Capricorn. One part of them will want to come out and experience the world. The inner self though will feel far more restricted and self-critical and will put a botch on any plans. It's not that humans have a dual personality; it's just that we must recognize that we are multi-faceted beings and our mental and emotional selves can be completely different.

In Astrology the Moon will change sign approximately every two days, so most of the time it's easy enough to find your Moon sign. Certain days, however, have the Moon changing sign, which can happen at any time of the day or night, so an accurate birth time is important.

In our example Jane Austen had Moon in Libra, and to all intents and purposes was obsessed with marriage. This was her Moon talking. Even though she did have two offers of matrimony, which she turned down, she never married. *"Anything is to be preferred or endured rather than marrying without Affection."*

This was not too much of a hardship for her as she had her Sun in the Fourth house and was happy as long as she had her family close.

The Dr Bach Flower Essences

In 1933 Dr Edward Bach, a medical doctor and Homeopath, published a little booklet called *The Twelve Healers and Other Remedies*. His theory was that if the emotional component a person was suffering from was removed, their 'illness' would also disappear. I tend to agree with this kind of thinking as most illnesses (except being hit by a car) are preceded by an unhappy event or an emotional disruption that then sets into place the body getting out of sync. Removing the emotional issue and bringing a bit of stability into someone's life, when they are 'all over the place', certainly doesn't hurt and in some cases can improve the overall health so much that wellness resumes.

Knowing which Bach Flower Essence can help certain worries and upsets gives your Sagittarius more control over their lives (and yours if you are in the vicinity) and I've quoted Dr Bach's actual words for each sign.

To use the Essences take 2 drops from the stock bottle and put them into a glass of water and sip. I tend to recommend putting them into a small water bottle, and sipping them throughout the day, at least 4 times. For young children, do the same.

Remember to seek medical attention if symptoms don't get better and/or seek professional counselling.

Aries Moon

"Courage is resistance to fear, mastery of fear, not absence of fear."
Mark Twain

As Aries is such a strong, confident sign and geared towards Looking After Number One, your Sagittarius with their Moon here (as it is also a Fire sign, so makes for double Fire) will enjoy stretching themselves and all around them. They will enjoy sports and being physically active. They will also not be shy in telling you exactly how they feel, so don't ask if you don't want the truth.

Bach Flower Essence Impatiens: *"Those who are quick in thought and action and who wish all things to be done without hesitation or delay."*

Taurus Moon

"I think everybody should have a great Wonderbra. There's so many ways to enhance them, everybody does it."
Christina Aguilera

As an Earth sign, Taurus is grounded in reality and enjoys life's physical pleasures. Food, chocolate, good wine, luxury and indulgence are not far away. Good sex will also be on the menu. Provided they have their finances in a stable manner, they will be full of life's joys. Poverty does not sit well with this combination, unless for spiritual purposes.

Bach Flower Essence Gentian: *"Those who are easily discouraged. They may be progressing well in the affairs of their daily life, but any small delay or hindrance to progress causes doubt and soon disheartens them."*

Gemini Moon

"My different personalities leave me in peace now."
Anna Freud

The Airy Gemini energy makes this the Moon that's happy to chat and change. They feel better when they have 50 projects on the go, some form of transport: bicycle, scooter, car or motorbike, so they can just 'pop out' when they need inspiration and access to ideas, books and magazines. Reading is a delight, being multi-lingual or having friends from diverse cultures all add up to a 'busy brain'. On a bad day the sign of the twins makes decisions difficult.

Bach Flower Essence Cerato: *"Those who have not sufficient confidence in themselves to make their own decisions."*

Cancer Moon

"I keep five really close friends. And I hang out with them. I think in LA, your friends become your family, and I've got a really good family here."
Jennifer Carpenter

The Water sign Cancer is concerned with 'Mum/Mom', home and the hearth. They feel better feeling nourished emotionally and physically. Family is important. Where they lay their hat is their home and they can struggle with their Sagittarius Sun wanting liberty and their Moon wanting dependency. As the Moon is in its 'natural' sign, they understand feelings, if only they'd slow down enough to feel them properly.

Bach Flower Essence Clematis: *"Living in the hopes of happier times, when their ideals may come true."*

Leo Moon

"Life is too short to be little. Man is never so manly as when he feels deeply, acts boldly, and expresses himself with frankness and with fervour."
Benjamin Disraeli

Do not ignore the Firey Moon in Leo, you'll be on shaky ground. They love an audience, the bigger the better! No shy, modest energies here. Red carpets, enthusiastic applause, recognition of their wonderful-ness. All praise will be appreciated. Warmth and friendliness are key attributes and as a Fixed sign, change might be more difficult.

Bach Flower Essence Vervain: *"Those with fixed principles and ideas, which they are confident are right."*

Virgo Moon

"I only get ill when I give up drugs."
Keith Richards

Ruled by chatty Mercury, Virgo Moon loves to communicate and as the sign of health and healing can become focused on their physical well-being. The two signs Virgo and Sagittarius are in a 'square aspect' = inner-conflict, so can work against feeling contented. There is always something niggling away at their psyche, worrying their inner mind. Relaxation and visualization work well to bring inner harmony.

Bach Flower Essence Centuary: *"Their good nature leads them to do more than their own share of work and they may neglect their own mission in life."*

Libra Moon

"The intuitions of all humanity declare that marriage can hold the greatest good in life."
Dion Fortune

Airy Libra is represented by the scales of justice, so a certain amount of indecision is found. One day up, the next down. Ruled by smoochy Venus, love and relationships are never far away. Having a compatible partner will/can become a life's mission, so date carefully to find 'The One'. Fairness is also very much a daily concern, so be sure to work with integrity.

Bach Flower Essence Scleranthus: *"Those who suffer from being unable to decide between two things, first one seeming right then the other."*

Scorpio Moon

"I've stopped caring about skeptics, but if they libel or defame me they will end up in court."
Uri Geller

Intense, watery Scorpio wants to find a truth they can trust. Once found, they will cling on forever, never swayed from their path. This is the Moon that wants to get to the depths of their feelings. Ruled by Pluto the transforming planet, keep in mind the words: deep, profound and meaningful and you'll have a better understanding of their motivations.

Bach Flower Essence Chicory: *"They are continually correcting what they consider wrong and enjoy doing so."*

Sagittarius Moon

"Learn about the world, the way it works, any kind of science and anthropology; it's really an interesting place we live in. Evolution is a really fantastic idea, even more than the idea of God I think."
Randy Newman

If you want the truth about something, ask a Sagittarius. If you want the truth, warts and all, ask a double Sagittarius. They won't be worried about what you think or do, they believe in their freedom as much as you believe in yours. Their turn of phrase will delight or destroy depending on your viewpoint. Firing their Jupiter inspired arrows into the distance is their true pleasure and you might just be inspired enough to join them.

Bach Flower Essence Agrimony: *"They hide their cares behind their humor and jesting and try to bear their trials with cheerfulness."*

Capricorn Moon

"I have never been a serious person... I am not serious at all because existence is not serious."
Bhagwan Shree Rajneesh

As a practical, serious Earth sign, a Capricorn Moon feels better when confronted with the reality of life, rather than the fluff. Maybe a more difficult Moon for a Sagittarius to have but one that has produced lasting success for Kim Basinger and Brad Pitt.

Capable of withstanding life's rocky complexities without succumbing to too much despair. When negativity strikes, fear can loom large, so aim for practical solutions.

Bach Flower Essence Mimulus: *"Fear of worldly things, illness, pain, accident, poverty, of dark, of being alone, of misfortune. They secretly bear their dread and do not speak freely of it to others."*

Aquarius Moon

"I want freedom and I realize that the only way to get it is to quit breaking the law."

Gary Gilmore

Ruled by wacky Uranus, the Airy Aquarius Moon wants independence and autonomy. Couple that with the Firey Sagittarius Sun and you've got someone who will travel to the ends of the earth to attain mental freedom. Don't crowd them in, or out, allow them space to breathe and 'be' and you'll have a happy, quirky individual.

Bach Flower Essence Water Violet: *"For those who like to be alone, very independent, capable and self-reliant. They are aloof and go their own way."*

Pisces Moon

"I truly am indeed, Alone again, naturally."

Gilbert O'Sullivan

The watery sensitive Pisces Moon is another conflicting square aspect for the Sagittarius Sun. Fairies, angels and mystical insights will be companions on their path. On a good day, they will light a flame for your eternal candle, on a bad day they will be hard to reach, wandering in Neptune's troubled waters.

Bach Flower Essence Rock Rose: *"For cases where there even appears no hope or when the person is very frightened or terrified."*

Chapter 5

The Houses

This is the bit of astrology that gets people the most confused. What is a house? Well, they were actually originally called mansions, as this is the place in the chart where the planets 'lived'. So if you imagine a house is the 'home' of a planet, you will understand things a little more. Depending on which house system you use, and most of the default computer applications use 'Placidus', the planets are placed mathematically around the circle. So if you have a certain Ascendant, your Sun will end up in a certain house in the Zodiac circle-map. The houses aren't a place in the sky; they're places in the map of the sky that we call a Birth Chart.

I use the Equal House System, as this is the easiest system to explain to clients and students as each house is the same equal size. It is also the oldest house system and my thoughts are: "If it ain't broke don't fix it!"

In our example Jane Austen has her Sun in the 4th house and as we will find, the 4th house is all about family, home and roots so the following quote from *Becoming Jane Austen* by Jon Spence really applies:

Jane Austen lived her entire life as part of a close-knit family.

I've also included what Ascendant each house position will/should have. My dad had a Sagittarius Ascendant and his Sun in the 1st house, which is what gave him his strong personality and forceful drive.

The First House, House of Personality

"I believe in opportunity. In optimism. In kindness. In wisdom. In consciousness. In natural justice. And in bloody hard work."
Jonathan Cainer

The first house is the place of the 'self' and 'Number One' so with the Sun here, the focus will mostly be self-assured and brave. There is also the tendency to tackle things quickly and decisively. Think of warriors-on-their-path and you'll have the right idea.
(Ascendant Capricorn or Sagittarius)

The Second House, House of Money, Material Possessions and Self-Worth

"Money? How did I lose it? I never did lose it. I just never knew where it went."
Edith Piaf

The second house emphasis is on the things we own and can possess, also how we feel about ourselves, so having the Sun here will make the native happier when money and possessions are safe.
(Ascendant Sagittarius or Scorpio)

The Third House, House of Communication & Short Journeys

"Animation can explain whatever the mind of man can conceive. This facility makes it the most versatile and explicit means of communication yet devised for quick mass appreciation."
Walt Disney

Communication and all things associated with it are important here. The third house moves on from the 'self' to the slightly wider idea of getting-on with those around us. With the Sun here, there is a need to be connected to others, rather than just existing in solitary confinement.

(Ascendant Scorpio or Libra)

The Fourth House, House of Home, Family & Roots

"There is nothing like staying at home for real comfort."
Jane Austen

The fourth house is where we feel nurtured by our closest family. Where we want to be with those who are closely connected to us. The Sun placed here will make the native more inclined to work-from-home or at the very least feel more comfortable there.

(Ascendant Libra or Virgo)

The Fifth House, House of Creativity & Romance

"I must create a system or be enslaved by another man's; I will not reason and compare: my business is to create."
William Blake

Now we have the need to show our 'work' to others. The fifth house concentrates on creation: by being artistic or by giving birth to children. The need is to be recognised for these creative efforts. Hiding away those creations is not an option.

(Ascendant Virgo or Leo)

The Sixth House, House of Work & Health

"There are a couple of people I would like to mention who are wonderful healers. I have seen both of them many times."
Paul Hewitt, Astrologer

The sixth house is where we self-heal, where our health is expressed and our daily work. All of the things that need active input. How we tackle the detail of these issues is through practical application.

(Ascendant Leo or Cancer)

The Seventh House, House of Relationships & Marriage

"Amour, amour, amour. Tout comme ça elle est. – Love, love, love. All like that she is."
Maurice Denis, Artist

Now we are concerned with 'others'. This is the home of relationships, personal and loving. With the Sun here, there is a need to be in a relationship, for better or worse. Love in all its guises will be a constant attraction.

(Ascendant Cancer or Gemini)

The Eighth House, House of Life Force in Birth, Sex, Death & After-Life

"If sex is such a natural phenomenon, how come there are so many books on how to do it?"
Bette Midler

The need to get deep and personal is displayed in the eighth house. It also governs sex and the after-life, so natives with their Sun here will have strong energies focused on their true desires. Once their minds are made up, nothing will stand in the way of attaining them.

(Ascendant Gemini or Taurus)

The Ninth House, House of Philosophy & Long Distance Travel

"I go to temple a lot less than I would like because, when I do, people still look at me as if they think it's a publicity stunt."
Sammy Davis, Jr

All forms of long-distance travel and the wider world are expressed in the ninth house. With the Sun here, philosophy and religion and the wider expanses of the mind are natural playmates.

(Ascendant Taurus or Aries)

The Tenth House, House of Social Identity & Career

"I'm a very determined businesswoman... I've got lots of things to do, and I don't have time to be classified as difficult."
Kim Basinger

The tenth house is where we want to be 'seen' by others, where we're aiming for in our career. With the Sun here, there is a big concern to make something of themselves and succeed.

(Ascendant Aries or Pisces)

The Eleventh House, House of Social Life & Friendships

"The monster was the best friend I ever had."
Boris Karloff

This is where we now need someone else to play with. Where friends are made and altruism prevails. Being part of a group or organisation that brings people together for a common purpose or idea/l is also on the agenda.

(Ascendant Pisces or Aquarius)

The Twelfth House, House of Spirituality

"I'm full of emotion and I want a release, and if you're on stage and if it's really working and you've got the audience with you, it's a oneness you feel."
Janis Joplin

Like Pisces the 12th sign of the Zodiac, the 12th house is concerned with spiritual matters. Where the soul needs to find its place and dreams and intuitions are a constant craving. Needing to be still is important as is meditation and dreaming and being able to express oneself through dreams is a must.

(Ascendant Aquarius or Capricorn)

Chapter 6

The Problems

Funnily enough, in the work that I do, I don't get too many people complaining about Sagittarians, but I do have a lot of Sagittarius clients. So most of the problems I encounter are with the Sagittarians themselves, rather than their friends, partners or children. Maybe this is because they are a Fire sign and Fire signs tend to want to sort things out rapidly? They are one of the more impatient signs, Leo and Aries being the others. Fire signs don't tend to wait a long time to 'sort something out' as they tend to want to get a resolution as quickly as possible.

Some of problems my Sagittarius clients come up against are mostly to do with them having vast ambitions that haven't yet been realized.

Sometimes Sagittarius can be a little impractical, which is part of the problem. Having great ideas is different from bringing them into reality. So I might see a Sagittarius in private practice who has a Grand Master Plan to become an accomplished healer, but they haven't quite finished the course they started, rented a room, bought any business cards or planned any marketing.

And it's very difficult to give any advice to a Sagittarius! This is because they already know all the answers and are too busy working on their Grand Master Plan to take any suggestions on board.

It's no good being subtle. It's no good dropping little hints. It's also no good being polite, reasonable, or understated. To get your point across, you really have to be like an Aries: direct, forceful and to-the-point.

Remember Mandi in Chapter One describing what makes her cross: *"people telling me what I can and can't do. Never tell me I can't do something."* She won't mind if she completely fails at something. She won't even mind if she falls flat on her face! She's used to these things and will just get up, brush herself off and carry on with whatever she was doing.

But I'm sure if you were to tell her *not* to do something, or order her to do something else, or make her feel guilty about something, that wouldn't work either.

Most of the Sagittarian clients I see in private practice also come to me to discuss their 'Life Path'. This is a very important Sagittarius ideal. They want to feel they are 'going in the right direction'.

What might blow them off course can be relationship break-ups (they generally tell me they're fine about it ending, then they complain they'll be 'on their own forever'...!), getting the sack or not having enough money to travel. Don't forget, clients generally only come and see me when things are bad. They don't ring me up to say: "I've won the lottery!"; it's mostly: "He/she has left me/I've left him/her, I've lost my job/relative, I'm going to leave him/her, I'm having an affair with him/her"... those sorts of things.

One thing to remember with a Sagittarius, if they feel bad about something in their life, they will generally want to relocate.

So, if they've been dumped, they'll want to go and live in Australia, Outer Mongolia, or somewhere miles away from where the trouble happened. So if a client has had a very challenging life and they're got a few planets in Gemini as well, I'll find they've moved house every time something upsetting has happened.

So here are a few examples of the sort of problems a Sagittarius may come across, or equally the relative/friend/ partner may find is happening:

My Sagittarius doesn't want to 'Settle Down'

This is the complaint that generally comes from a Water sign. If you're a Cancer, you will have to accept your Sagittarius might never want to 'settle' down in the way you've been imagining. They won't want to have your names embroidered on the towels, or go around the supermarket choosing vegetables for dinner; they also won't want to wear fluffy slippers and relax for hours in front of the TV:

> *"Sitting in front of the TV, or not leaving my backyard, makes me wiggy, and promotes a certain kind of anxiety. Without exploration, from time to time, without expanding my view, I'm left with a sense of stagnation."*

Marie, Sagittarius Ascendant, Sun in the 1st

Sagittarian Brad Pitt, Sagittarius Ascendant, Sun in the 1st and Moon in Capricorn is a classic example of the Sagittarian's marriage complexities. He was married for 5 years to Jennifer Aniston who is Sun Aquarius in the 4th, Libra Ascendant, Moon in Sagittarius, so you can see there were astrological connections with her Moon and his Sun.

While they were divorcing he began a relationship with Angelina Jolie, who is a Gemini, Sun in the 11th, Cancer Ascendant and Moon in Aries. As I am writing this, they are still together and so far have six children. Three who were adopted, one set of twins (boy/girl) and one daughter .To make up a truly international family, their adoptive children were born in Cambodia, Ethiopia and Vietnam, their daughter was born in Namibia and their twins were born in Nice, France. As you can tell from this little summary, Brad isn't bothered about 'convention'.

In an interview in the Daily Telegraph he said: *"We're a very nomadic family, and it works for us."*[7]

Being settled (Taurus territory) or snuggled-up (Cancer

territory) or being jealous of their friends/ex-lovers (Scorpio territory) will just make your Sagittarius head for the door. Suggesting a quick trip to Europe or travelling with some friends to Machu Picchu will put a smile on their face and you'll hear the sound of the suitcase being packed. They won't want to 'settle' down in any conventional sense. They might even marry more than once. Go back and read Chapter One and remind yourself of their motivating characteristics and you'll understand why.

My Sagittarius has got into a fight with their Mother/Father/Sibling and wants me to take sides

If your family comprises of lots of Fire signs you're going to find this will happen. There's not much you can do other than offer a sympathetic ear. Don't take sides but reassure your Sagittarius that you believe in them and change the subject. If they're so wound up that they are considering legal action, tell them to get a second opinion and try and distract them while things calm down. The best way to tackle an overdose of Fire Sign energy is to walk away from confrontation.

I once did a reading for a Sagittarius lady who was a twin. Her (slightly older by minutes) sister and she never saw eye-to-eye and when they were children her older sister would torment her physically. She could never understand why, with them being identical twins. They had now completely separated and lived in totally different countries. She had a lot of anger towards her sister.

So, I calculated their respective charts and found out that even though they were twins, with the same Sun and Moon signs the Rising sign/Ascendant was different. The older sister had Aquarius Ascendant, Sun in the 10th and my client had Pisces Ascendant, Sun in the 9th. The older sister concentrated on her career and the younger liked travelling (!) hence her being in my office in the UK even though she was born and lived in the USA. When I could demonstrate to her that she was *different* to her sister and had no need to think she was the same... she felt a great sense of relief.

My Sagittarius wants to start up another company/business but they've already got two on the go

This does happen rather a lot. More than most signs Sagittarius loves to be self-employed. They love being their own boss (unless they've got a cautious streak) and they're not very good at knowing when to stop. They'll start one company up, then start another and before you know it, they're not just running one little business, they're selling a range of products/offering a multitude of services... and doing them all badly. I've seen this so many times, I don't care who I upset by telling you.

Your Sagittarius might not know when to stop, or when they're on to a good thing. They can completely ignore the finances of what they're involved in and borrow loads of money... and get deeper and deeper into debt, meanwhile you don't have enough money to eat, let alone send your kids to posh private school. Insist they cut back to the things they enjoy doing, and those that make the best money. The other little 'projects' can go on the back burner.

I was listening to an interesting radio programme about Winston Churchill's life while writing this. Inspirational man that he was, he also spent loads of money and lived 'like a king', gambled and swung from joy to despair coupled with wild spending habits.[6] As he was married to an Aries (fighting spirit) this wasn't too much of a problem and they stayed together.

So if your Sagittarius wants to start another business, try and persuade them to sit down, calmly and cost everything out. After spending a few hours with the calculator, they'll happily get back to the fun things, and you can breathe a sigh of relief. Stand up for yourself on this point. Bankruptcy is not attractive.

My Sagittarius wants to go/back to College/Uni/School to study for a PHD/Doctorate/Diploma/Higher Qualification/Degree but doesn't have any money/time

Now this problem is one a Sagittarius would never perceive as a problem. They like studying. They enjoy learning about things they're interested in and that's that.

If you're an Earth sign, this might make you nervous as you will be concerned about nice practical things such as 'enough money' and 'paying the bills'. These aren't top priority for a Sagittarius, so my suggestion would be to let it happen, provided it doesn't cost *you* any money. If they are funding themselves, all fine and dandy; but if they want you to pay the fees, or sell your car to help out, say "No!" very firmly. There are always other ways to get funded to study without having to go broke. You could get them to apply for a grant, or write to a charity or if they're a member of a professional society or organisation, they might have bursaries they could tap into. Their present employer might even help out. All they have to do is ask. Whatever you do, don't even try to prevent them when they've got this idea in mind. You'll push them further away, unless of course you want the relationship to end.

Chapter 7

The Solutions

OK, now you will have an idea of how to make a chart, the Sun placement your Sagittarius has, and their Moon sign, so you'll be well on the way to understanding them better. You'll also be living in a state of complete harmony all round.

No?

Don't despair.

It can take some time to get on with someone well. It also takes time to learn about the true motivations of a Sagittarius. Try not to rush the process. Think of it as a learning path, and you're exploring the wonders of the Universe, with someone else, who's excited about that Universe.

To assist your process, keep in mind two useful additions to your Tool Box of Solutions:

1) The wonderful self-help technique EFT: Emotional Freedom Technique
2) The Bach Flower Essences mentioned earlier for each Moon sign

I will now share with you the sort of things that upset a Sagittarius.

Here we have Sophie. A single Mum in her early 40's she practices as an alternative therapist and works from home so she can home-school her children.

She has a Leo Ascendant, so she likes to shine and isn't shy or retiring… normally. Sun in Sagittarius in the 4th house, so home comforts are important and Moon in Capricorn, so she has a tendency to be very self-critical and stern with her 'inner-child'.

She came to see me because she felt cross and we went through what that 'crossness' was about:

"I feel very, very anxious, angry, stressed-out and I feel INVADED," she said. *"I have to protect myself."*

I asked her what she was anxious about:

"Everything. I'm getting panic attacks, I feel suffocated, I'm worried about the houses, the crash, and my parent's disapproval. I'm worrying about the children and money."

I asked her to tell me more.

"It's my parents. They are giving with one hand, and taking with the other. Mum's been jumping around. She had some oil delivered and paid for it, then made a fuss when it cost £159. She kept saying it was too dear, then kept telling me to use it to warm the house. I feel embarrassed and humiliated. I feel so angry because she's being 'so nice' but she's making me a 'poor thing project'."

Sophie was angry that her mother was taking control of her life and making decisions without her approval. She's a grown woman but her mother was treating her like a child.

*"I told my bloke to b***** off, but he won't take the hint."* (He's Aries with Aquarius Moon and Leo Ascendant too). *"I don't need him, he's wanting all my energy. I really lost it. I feel invaded. I have no room of my own, no home of my own, no privacy. Every day I feel exhausted and invaded. It's the humiliation of it all, I'm made to feel stupid and I feel unvalued."*

It transpired that Sophie's mother was phoning her everyday but it made Sophie feel as if her mother didn't trust her. Her boyfriend wanted to spend more much time with her, and had moved in, so her sense of freedom had also been completely lost.

This all was a recipe for disaster. A mother of a Sagittarius disapproving of the way her daughter was bringing up her children. Not actually saying anything to her face, but tut-tutting and making derogatory remarks and delivering things without notice.

Oh dear!

A few days later Sophie rang to say the remedy I'd given her had helped, she was feeling less angry and was beginning to calm down.

To get on well with the Sagittarius in your life, you will need to develop certain understandings and no small amount of patience. If you're a Water or Earth sign you might get exasperated with their endless enthusiasm for life and their fun outlook.

If you feel you don't know how to help them tackle their present crisis, have a read through the various chart combinations and choose the one closest to your Sagittarian's make-up.

Aries Ascendant or Moon

If your Sagittarius is upset you're going to have to be quick here, because this sign combination moves fast. Here they will need some action. Aries is ruled by the planet Mars so the best solution for an upset Sagittarian with such a strong Ascendant is to get them out of the house, for a LONG walk. Talking about this won't wash. The Aries Ascendant will want ACTION (as opposed to Leo who wants CAMERA! ACTION!). Tai-chi class, Judo, running, fencing, action-based sports. Not competitive as this combination is likely to bop you on the head if they don't get their way, and this book is written to help the Sagittarian friend…

Taurus Ascendant or Moon

Now the energies are slower. To help your Sagittarius feel better get some cakes (low fat, sugar free) out of the cupboard. Listen for a few minutes, then get them booked in for a holisitic, healing, gentle aromatherapy massage. Sooner rather than later. Taurus wants basic needs met and those needs are food, sex, and skin. The BODY is important here.

Gemini Ascendant or Moon

Get the kettle on. Get the books out. Quote the Bible (either version, they're both good). Have the books to hand. Discuss. Discuss some more. Look at workable solutions. Listen. Nod your head every now and then. Smile. Look confident and speak as if you know how they are feeling/thinking. Take them for a short, local drive in the car and they'll soon spill the beans. The motion and interest brought with a short car or bike journey will get them back on track and fretting less.

Cancer Ascendant or Moon

Oodles of sympathy is needed here. Cancer is a Water sign, and unlike their Fire Sign Sun, makes a person who really needs EMPATHY. You can't just cluck and look interested here. Unless you have suffered what Cancer has, you're out of the game. Best strategy is to (again) get on the kettle, turn off your mobile, look calm and sympathetic, lean into the Cancer's space, mirror body language, and get the tissues handy. Cancers need to cry and will generally feel much better afterwards.

Leo Ascendant or Moon

The Second Fire sign of the Zodiac. You'd never guess it though because Leo thinks they are special and unique and need lots and lots of attention. "There, there, there" works well. So does "How can I help, what can I DO?". The Fire signs like action, Aries likes physical action, Sagittarius likes BIG VISTA action while Leo likes company action. They want an audience to demonstrate and act out their story to. The more the merrier! You won't want tissues, Leo has to be really suffering to cry and they tend to do so in the quiet and alone.

Virgo Ascendant or Moon

Now, I was tempted to say get the doctor round as Virgo is so concerned with their health. When upset though, a Virgo/ Sagittarius will fret, and fret and fret so you feel like screaming: "CALM DOWN". This isn't a helpful strategy but does come to mind when you've heard EVERY little detail of whatever was happening. If only they'd see that, and instead of fretting about their own health, they could be healing themselves or others. Virgo/Sagi won't really want to talk, as talking makes them feel worse. They will take a flower essence, Centuary is good or the Homeopathic remedy Ignatia. Emotional upsetments will also affect a Virgo/Sagi's physical health and they'll get tummy troubles, or asthma or a whole host of seemingly unrelated health conditions, when what they really need to do is lie down in the quiet and turn their brains off for a while.

Libra Ascendant or Moon

Here you might need the tissues again. You will also need calm and tranquil pleasant surroundings. Libra/Sagi is very sensitive to their environment and as Libra is 'ruled' by Venus they respond better to beauty and harmony. They might need gentle questioning, having tea is good but far better would be a big bunch of roses or a gentle aromatherapy massage. Things need to be balanced for Libra/Sagi and fair. Everyone has to take a share of what is going on. Point out that if they consider everyone else's point of view, they will only tire themselves even more, so it would be best to find just one strategy to 'move forward' with.

Scorpio Ascendant or Moon

Not much is going to be visible with this combination. They feel things so deeply and intensely that if you were capable of seeing what they were feeling, you'd be a bit shocked. Dark colours, blood red, deep yearnings. The solution is to allow them plenty of space. Yards of it. Somewhere where they can brood and ponder and yearn without it sucking everything in like a black hole. There is not much you can do to 'help' as they will prefer to lose themselves in the emotion. They might write a song or a poem or get horribly drunk.They might want revenge so be watchful of this and aware that if there are other people involved when a Scorpio/Sagi is worked-up, heads might roll. One useful tip is to get your Scorpio/Sagi to write a letter to the person/s concerned, then ritualistically burn it. Doing radical things like this will help considerably.

Sagittarius Ascendant or Moon

If you can visit a church or spiritual retreat, or you know a Tibetan monk or two, it will help things considerably. Sagittarius needs to understand the spiritual whys and wherefores. Like Gemini Moon the Bible is good but anything by a divine adept will make a double Sagittarius give some meaning to their circumstances. The Dalai Lama, the Buddha, ancient philosophical texts, any religion/nationality will do, the more exotic and challenging the better... dig them out and get your Sagi to read them. Oh, and they might make some very personal remarks while they're struggling, just ignore them!

Capricorn Ascendant or Moon

Be practical, realistic and get the dry sense of humour dusted off. This combination responds well to 'old fashioned' good humour. Maybe slapstick, maybe old funnies. First off get everything that has gone wrong into some sort of sensible perspective. Talk about the real things, the money, the plans, the future. Once they have a clear future-based goal, they cheer-up enormously. You will have to discuss the truth and not hide behind niceties. Libra combi's are happy for everyone to get on, Capricorn combi's will prefer one solution, one winner, one loser. They'd (obviously) prefer not to be the loser, but generally, in life, they don't expect much, so are rarely disappointed. They just expect everything to get worse. Try and guide them towards the idea that it is OK to have fun and enjoy life...

Aquarius Ascendant or Moon

Any major charity being mentioned will always help as Aquarius is the sign of autonomy and benefiting 'mankind'. I once recommended to a client, who had a Moon in Aquarius in his life, to give money to her favourite charity, as that would help her understand how devoted he was to her. If you can bring the wider world into the equation, so much the better. Make sure their sense of freedom and individuality hasn't been removed and correct any signs that it may have as otherwise you'll have a total breakdown on your hands.

Pisces Ascendant or Moon

This is the sign combination of sensitivity. Please be gentle with them. Imagine they are beings with gossamer wings, angels in disguise, beings from another planet and you'll have more of an idea of how to help them. They won't really listen to what you tell them, they'll sense it, but you might feel that nothing sank in. It did. It will just take a while to filter through all the other 'stuff' that is in their heads. Light a candle, burn incense, lay out some Angel Cards or use some other form of divination to help you. The I Ching is good and I know Sagittarians with this combi who will believe the 'oracle' more than the letter from the bank or the discussion with a trusted friend. So learn a little psychic technique or two and use them to assist you both.

Chapter 8

Believing In Tactics

Now I apologise for leaving until the final chapter my thoughts about belief and the Sagittarius ideal. First of all we need a definition.

My trusty Oxford Dictionary of Current English defines Belief as: *"act of believing"*.

OK, not helpful, so let's look at Believe: *"accept as true or as conveying truth"*.

Now here we come to truth and for a Sagittarius it's more than truth, it is...

TRUTH

They have their own code in life that they follow, their own belief/s and unlike other star signs unless you believe *in* their beliefs, you're standing alone on the pavement, with your Sagittarius running away. You need to believe *in* them, not just believe them and I'll explain the difference.

To believe someone goes like this:

Little Johnny gets home from school, covered in mud and with holes in his trousers. He tells you that he went to play football after school with his friends and he 'accidently' fell in the mud. You believe him, you know that what he's saying matches with some sort of truth as you can see the mud, the holes in the knees of his trousers where he fell over... it makes sense. This is not believing *in* Johnny, it's just straight belief.

Now think about Edith Piaf, the woman with the wonderful voice and strong personality. My dad was a big fan of hers, she was called 'the little sparrow' as she was discovered busking on the streets of Paris. She wanted you to believe *in* her. She wanted you to listen to the words of her famous song *Non, Je Ne Regrette Rien*…

(I can still sing it myself, I heard my dad sing it so much.)

She wanted you to believe *in* her, to believe in her as an individual person but part of the human race. As someone who had come from a poor background, who loved her country, who didn't care what the authorities thought of her. She wanted you to believe *in* her. To know that the words she was saying were *her* truth.

She wanted your trust, your whole-hearted support, for you to be looking at the same wide, expansive vista of the beautiful world we inhabit.

Imagine standing on the top of a highest mountain, looking at a breath-taking view around you of hills and lakes and rocks and you can see far, far into the distance, almost to the ends of the earth… that's what a Sagittarius wants in your belief *of* them, your belief *in* them.

To believe in their personal world they have created, that is fun and exciting, that involves travel and a higher state of being, that has a 'wow' factor. They want you to follow the same dream that they are following. They want you as an equal. Not as a leader, not as a 'fan' (that's more Leo territory), they don't want you to worship them, or even worship the same 'god' as them, they don't want you to agree with them either, they just want you to challenge and excite them with the wonderfulness that is in the world, that does exist.

They want you to 'have faith in the existence of… ', then fill in the blanks. They want you to have faith in their beliefs. And we're not talking religion here, faith is with a small 'f'.

Here is a Sagittarius man trying to describe what he means when he's talking about his sign. What he'd like people to understand about him:

Well 'Truth' and also when people say 'Meaning' when talking about us. For me, meaning is the driving force and then some behind my overall philosophical outlook. There is a meaning behind everything, and we care to find out exactly what it is.

So behind the belief is some meaning, and isn't that really what most of us are looking for? A Life Led With Meaning. I don't think you need to be Sagittarius to want that, but they will want it like it's a life and death situation. The more you talk or write about 'higher truths' the more you get away from reality and since this is a practical book to help people who know or are friends with Sagittarius, I won't take this much further.

Just remember, they want you to believe *in* them, not just believe them.

Now on the other side of the discussion is religious belief. It's a vast subject and one that can precipitate big changes in people's lives.

Here's Tina Turner talking to Oprah about her experiences of Buddhist chanting:

The women who sold drugs to Ike said, "What are you doing here, Tina? How can you live with this madness?" Then one day, someone told me, "Buddhism will save your life." I was willing to try anything. I started to chant. Once, I chanted, went to the studio, and put down a vocal, just like that. Ike was so excited that he gave me a big wad of money and said, "Go shopping!" I thought, "This chanting stuff works." I was hooked. I still believe in the Lord's Prayer. I find a form of the Lord's Prayer in Buddhism. Every religion has rules for living a good life. If you practice any kind of spirituality, it moves you to stages where you gather other ways of communicating. I never close a door on any other religion. Most of the time, some part of it makes sense to me. I don't believe everyone has to chant just because I chant. I believe all religion is about touching something inside of yourself. It's all one thing. If we would realize this, we could make a change in this millennium.

Your Sagittarius Boss

"It is my belief you cannot deal with the most serious things in the world unless you understand the most amusing."
Winston Churchill

As I'm self-employed, I don't have a boss but in the past I worked in a job as a receptionist for a company that sold, imported and distributed skateboarding/kiting and mostly male/teen products and one of the partners was a Sagittarius. We got on well.

He had an enormous appetite for doing exciting things. He also drank SO much coffee that I got worried for his health but he sort of bounced around the office, getting into deep discussions about the next line of products. One of my jobs was to book his plane tickets and he was never happier than when he'd got something booked and was going out to 'meet' someone and try out their latest gadget.

They sold a wide range of what can only be described as adult toys. Things like the 'stomp rocket' where you had a plastic bulb that you 'stomped' on and it sent a jet of air into a little launch pad that sent your foam 'rocket' into the air. We used one when my son was little in our local park and we had a line of kiddies who wanted to take a turn and send the rocket up in the air. Kept a bunch of kids amused for hours...

My boss would get grumpy if people weren't on his side and continually challenged and argued with his partner, who was a Gemini. They were like a married couple and every now and then there would be an enormous argument about something or other, and one of them would burst out of the meeting room, in a blaze of emotion, vowing to never talk to the other again. And a few hours later you'd find them in the stockroom, playing with a yo-yo or some other weird new invention and debating the pros and cons of it, as if nothing had happened earlier.

Underneath the adult exterior was a happy, inspired child that just enjoyed playing.

Sagittarius love of personal freedom can inspire them to become entrepreneurs, as they are defined as taking a chance with 'profit or loss'. This sits well with the Sagittarian not being bothered about failing. If their dream is big enough, they'll just try another tack.

Two such people come to mind: J Paul Getty; Capricorn Ascendant, Sun in the 12th and Moon in Scorpio, who made his millions in the oil business and Ann Souter Gloag, Moon in Capricorn, who founded a bus company called 'Gloag Trotter' that later became 'Stagecoach'. In their cases the Capricorn sternness and forward focus helped them 'stay the course'.

So, to get on well with your Sagittarius boss, don't bother arguing with them, unless it's something you feel passionate about. Your passion just might rub off on them. Don't restrict their personal freedom and keep in mind that their honesty might make things awkward occasionally but will all blow over in minutes. They will reward you generously if they can witness your enthusiasm for what you do and most of the time they'll leave you to your own devices. They are also unlikely to breathe down your neck or correct any mistakes you make.

Your Sagittarius Child

Time and again I hear in private practice stories from unhappy Sagittarians who felt their parents just didn't understand them.

If we go back to the Sagittarius keywords that reflect their driving forces – Adventurous, Philosophical, Independent – we can understand that reining in those rather strong forces is going to be tricky. How do you help a child that's interested in vast concepts and assist them in developing them rather than suffocating their enthusiasm?

Maybe the best approach is to give them a certain amount of freedom of expression but just keep a beady eye on them 'going too far'... as the natural instinct of a Jupiter-ruled child is to 'overdo' things.

Here we have Sam who is a computer wizard and lives in Connecticut, USA:

No parent is perfect, and their biggest mistake, I realize now, was out of their love for me and without realizing, it did more harm than good. Growing up, my Sag Sun/Aries moon wanted nothing more than to be FREE – to go out and play with other kids, to party as a teenager, to make my own mistakes, to have fun, to perform! But I didn't get to do any of that – in fact, I never even learned how to ride a bike, because we weren't allowed outside (too dangerous) and we weren't allowed to hang out with friends (bad influences and their families can't be trusted). I wasn't encouraged nor supported in my desire to get into the performing arts, even though it always has and probably always will be my biggest passion, because they felt that wasn't a respectable line of work and they wanted better for me.

*Most parents teach their children to just "be yourself" but growing up in my house, we were taught the exact opposite. "Be perfect" instead. Whenever we had company over the house, my mother would go completely OCD with cleaning, cleaning like a manic every nook and cranny, to the point where the house looked like a museum, not a place to live, and my sisters and I had to dress up and be on our absolute best behaviour, not making a peep when the guests were over. We came off as perfectly neat, clean, pretty, polite, the perfect family to outsiders, but it wasn't until the company left that we could relax and let our hair down and act like our true selves. So having people over was always a burden for my sisters and I, because it meant that we had to put on a show. If one hair was out of place, it was a HUGE DEAL to my mother. So again, she meant well, but it backfired. My 'true' self IS a **Sagittarius** – I want to laugh and dance and make jokes and burp and not care if one hair is out of place on my head – but I've never done that before.*

I loved the bit at the end where he said he wanted to "make jokes and burp and not care if one hair is out of place." Wonderful! If that doesn't describe the true Sagittarius spirit, I don't know what does.

Now, just to differentiate with the Aquarius love of freedom, their freedom is to 'think' whatever they like... while the Sagittarius freedom is to 'do' whatever they like. Not to be destructive or difficult, but to feel their bodies are free to explore that exciting planet we live in. So, your Sagittarius child might enjoy some sport of some kind. I know lots of Sagittarius females who love horse riding. Maybe it's the Sagittarius image of half-man half-centaur, or just the fact that for some people riding a horse can make them feel alive and free?

One thing is for sure, if you want your Sagittarius child to be eternally happy don't restrict them too much. Don't burst their bubbles or dampen their creativity. Celebrate and enjoy with them the wonders they discover.

Your Sagittarius (female) Lover

If you keep in mind the keywords we used earlier about Sagittarius: adventurous, philosophical, independent and... tactless, you will understand how it's not quite so easy to date a Sagittarius female.

The Sagittarius women that I know personally and in private practice have often said to me that they're not 'looking' for a partner, they're just hoping that one will turn up. And since you can't really tell a Sagittarius what to do, or make any suggestions that they are going to listen to, helping them find a partner is the complex challenge!

Their love of independence is a major feature. This is different from Aquarius love of freedom. An Aquarius needs mental freedom, Sagittarius needs literal freedom. The freedom to explore the vast expanses of the world and other cultures. As they enjoy travelling so much, their partner must also love travelling too.

Here we have Amy describing what she's looking for in her ideal partner. She tells us a little about herself first:

My life is an open book, honesty is my game and I expect the same from others. I'm no shrinking violet so don't put me in the corner! I'm open to most life experiences. I love adventures, big or small and rarely plan ahead. Although I'm independent I love male company, I want a companion who wants to be my equal, not dominate me or wither under me.

Intense? Maybe.

Fun? Yes.

Serious? When called for.

Stupid? Not!

Looking for? Hmmmm, well that's a difficult one. I want a man, masculine, not vain. Someone I can look up to and not wither under. I dislike wimpy but also dislike being bossed about. I want a partner that I can talk to, discuss things with, have a debate but not an argument. I want someone who is impulsive, but dependable. Fun but serious when called for. Intelligent but not condescending. Cultured but not anal. Am I looking for a fairy tale? Challenge me!

If we decipher what she is actually saying, she's looking for 'true' male spirit. She's also looking for someone who will be her equal and not expect her to obey or concede. There would have to be a certain amount of educational intelligence as she's asking for a 'debate' not an 'argument'. If we are thinking in astrological terms, Amy is looking for an Aries, a fellow Fire sign who will not be shy and will also be capable of shrugging off that 'honesty' (which can actually translate into tactlessness).

Britney Spears, Libra Ascendant, Sun in the 3rd, Moon in Aquarius, has the typical Sagittarian dilemma of wanting to find her 'Prince Charming' but equally spending months of the year on tour. With her Sun and Moon in two freedom-loving signs, she's going to need a partner who can fulfil her dreams of independence, a hard combination to pull off. Not impossible but more difficult.

The Universe won't just suddenly send you your ideal partner if you're off travelling so much. It's hard to hit a moving target! The US actress Bette Midler, Aries Ascendant, Sun in the 8th, Moon in Scorpio is, at the moment, married:

Marriage is such hard work. And it's full of rage and real human drama. Every day is a struggle. My husband and I are having a good year, but the first years were truly terrible. We got married, and then we realized we had very different opinions about a lot of things. But this year we had a breakthrough. In a marriage, you struggle and struggle and struggle, and then you realize that you have to ride the horse in the direction it's going. You stop trying to pull the reins in another direction. My husband already knows that stuff. But for me, it was the whole square-peg-in-a-round-hole thing. Finally, I said to myself, "This would be so much nicer if..."
Let him be. That was my mother's big line in Yiddish. She used to say to my father all the time, "Leave 'em alone! Let 'em be!"

That Aries Ascendant really doesn't like subtlety and with Moon in Scorpio *and* her Sun in the 8th she needs to feel trusted and secure. Let's hope she finds it!

You will have to have a strong personality to successfully date a Sagittarius female. You will have to have the courage of your convictions, an in-date passport, a good working knowledge of current affairs and not be possessive or needy. You will also have to allow her to have her 'own space' in whatever way she feels comfortable.

Your Sagittarius (male) Lover

I sometimes think, the only way to truly learn about how someone views themselves is to read a profile that they write about themselves... and no better place to find these things out is on the dating websites.

Most people know that to 'attract a partner' you have to write about your good points, obviously not your bad and it is in this spirit that I include an anonymous poster's description of himself.

Mr X lives in London, was born in 1973 and is single. Here he describes what he is looking for and, girls, make a mental note. What someone writes is almost as important as what they don't write.

When asked "What are you looking for?" notice that he gives much more than one option, in fact he's obviously ticked every box:

Activity partners; Friends; Let's see what happens; A short-term relationship; A long-term relationship; Marriage; A fling

He is NOT looking to have a ring on his finger, his slippers under the sofa and monogamy. Notice he puts 'marriage' second last on the last. His first choice is 'activity partners', which makes sense as he lists his sports interests as:

Camping; Cycling; Horse Riding; Extreme sports; Golf; Hiking; Mountain biking; Running; Rock climbing; Sailing; Scuba diving; Skiing; Snowboarding; Squash; Swimming; Walking; Water skiing; Weight training; Hang- /Paragliding; Yoga

So, if you're a Cancer or Scorpio or Capricorn, you could find his changeability and need-to-be-doing-something very tiring.

He also has NOT written that he is looking for true love. This is NOT his highest priority, so, girls, once again, don't date a Sagittarius if you're looking for a quick, swift waltz down the aisle.

He is also bilingual, has never smoked and went to University, so already we're looking at a typical Sagittarius man... he even says this himself:

I'm a typical Sagittarius; optimistic, open, honest and loyal, though at times self-indulgent, demanding and self-assertive. Although a complete I, I live the philosophy 'carpe diem' and love it when life brings happy coincidences to those who are aware and not sleep-walking through their lives. Life for me is nothing without spontaneity and adventure, whilst keeping a strong grip on what's important to me: love, commitment, loyalty, self-awareness.

I'm looking for a woman who feels the same, can keep pace and doesn't take herself too seriously.

One who's strong and conservative enough to rein in my impulsiveness whilst liberal enough not to suppress my creativity. If I sound like a handful, I probably am, but then like everything in life, unless it challenges you it's probably not worth doing...

I have a dry sense of humour, a strong sense of irony, and my sarcasm knows no bounds. Please feel free to laugh at me, be able to laugh at yourself and join me at laughing at the crazy world we live in...

Not known for my diplomacy, it's probably best that you know up front that I'm honest to a fault and can be ruthlessly tactless, though my natural charm and winning smile always make up for any offence I may cause... "

Then he tells us a little about what he's actually looking for, and as I pointed out in *How to Bond with an Aquarius*, most people think they are 'looking for' someone just like them. Who have the same interests, like the same food, live the same life... but as you can appreciate, after a while all that sameness could get boring...

Anyway, what a man *says* they are looking for tends to tell you a lot about *them*, but nothing about *you*.

He's not bothered about location, so even if you live in Tristan da Cunha (small island in the southern Atlantic Ocean, population 271 people) that won't deter him from dating you, provided you meet the specifications.

He wants someone a *maximum* of one year older than him, could be a lot younger, with a body-type of *Slim; Average; Athletic; Curvaceous;* who doesn't have any children already but *might* want some later, and he's not at all bothered about education, ethnicity, income, religion or language. NONE of those things would be a barrier to meeting/dating him. The foods he likes are: *British; French; Greek; Indian; Japanese; Italian; Seafood; Sushi; Thai; Vegetarian.*

It was interesting to note his profile hardly contained ANY details about what he was looking for, so to date this man successfully, you'd have to be confident in yourself and not worried about what he gets up to. Cosy domesticity was not on his profile. He also has an incredibly busy life, with hobbies and reading... and his job in the film industry. So, if you want to date him, your life would have to be equally busy, otherwise you'd be at home, waiting for him to contact you... and you might have a long wait.

I also asked Victoria, an Aries lady in her 50s, living a 'comfortable lifestyle' in Los Angeles, a few questions about her Sagittarius husband. They have both been married before and have six children between them. They built a house on a small island in the Caribbean, where they spend a lot of their time. Michael is in his late 60's and I asked Victoria what attracted her to her life companion.

We met at the United Lodge of Theosophists. We had known each other for years, but didn't really get to know each other well until we co-moderated a class together. After that, one thing led to another.

The things that attracted me to him were his sense of humor, and the facility with which you can have a conversation with him. He is very knowledgeable in several subjects and has a natural gift of the gab. As a result he can also be something of a know-it-all. Sometimes

I feel as if he is too impressionable, and so can be convinced that things are true without thoroughly exploring where it's coming from. This is strange to me, because as a business owner and salesman, he himself has the capacity to sell ice to Greenlanders.

However, basically he is a left-wing-progressive-liberal, though he occasionally will argue a libertarian point of view (sometimes I think to just be contrary). He believes in the law of Karma, though sometimes he can be judgmental in his estimation of its effects (if something bad happens, the individual must have done something to bring it on!). Yet he will be the first person to contribute to a cause, or speak out against injustice. He believes in reincarnation and the evolution of the soul. He has no attraction to conventional religion. Like many Sags he thinks very highly of himself. For instance, he is quite convinced that Sagittarius is a much superior sign to other signs. I cringe when he offers his crack astrological assessment of people's signs.

So, to successfully date a Sagittarius, make sure you keep those ideas of freedom, your and theirs, firmly in mind.

What to do when your Sagittarius relationship has ended

One thing is for sure, a Sagittarius relationship that's destined to end won't end slowly. One day you'll be together, the next day the bags will be packed and you'll be on your own. There also won't be any subtle lead-up, or chance to reconcile. Their Fiery spirit will be rushing off to new horizons, maybe into the arms of someone else, more likely to be prompted by the eternal search for freedom.

Fire Sign

If you're a Fire sign: Aries, Leo or Sagittarius and you are now in the aftermath of the relationship my best advice is to use the Element you're ruled by, which will be fire. Now I'm not suggesting that you tear up all their clothes and make a bonfire in the garden, or set alight to their favourite books. No, we're going to do something much more empowering.

Get a candle, any type will do but the best would be a small nightlight and light it and recite:

"I... (your name) do let you... (Sagittarius name) go, in freedom and with love so that I am free to attract my true soul-love."

Leave the candle in a safe place to burn down, at least an hour's worth of burn time is good. Be careful not to leave the house and keep an eye on it.

Then over the next few days, gather up any belongings that are your (now) ex-Sagittarian's and either leave them round your ex's house, or give them to charity.

If you have any photos, don't be in a big rush to tear them all up, as some Fire signs are prone to, then years later, when they feel better about the situation, regret not having any reminders of nice times you may have had. When you have the strength, keep a few of the nicer photos, and discard the rest.

Earth Sign

If you are an Earth sign: Taurus, Virgo or Capricorn you will feel less inclined to do something drastic or outrageous (unless of course you have a Fire sign Moon...)

The end of your relationship should involve the Element of Earth and this is best tackled using some trusty crystals.

The best ones to use are the ones associated with your Sun sign and also with protection. The following crystals are considered protective but are also birth stones (pages 188-192 *Cunningham's Encyclopedia of Crystal, Gem and Metal Magic*, by Scott Cunningham):[8]

Taurus = Emerald

Virgo = Agate

Capricorn = Onyx

Take your crystal and cleanse it in fresh running water. Wrap it in some tissue paper then take yourself on a long walk into the country. When you find a suitable spot, dig a small hole and place the crystal in the ground.

Think about how your relationship has ended. Remember the good times and the bad. Forgive yourself for any mistakes you think you may have made. Then imagine a beautiful plant growing where you have buried the crystal and the plant blossoming and growing strong. This represents your new love that will be with you when the time is right.

Air Sign

If you are an Air sign: Gemini, Libra or Aquarius you might want to talk about what happened first before you feel happy enough to end your connection. Air signs need reasons and answers and can waste precious life-energy looking for those answers. Forgive yourself first of all for the relationship ending. It's no one's fault and time will heal the wounds. When you are having a better day and your thoughts are clear, get a piece of paper and write your (ex) Sagittarius a letter.

This isn't a letter you are actually going to post, so you can be as honest as you want with your thoughts.

Write to them thus:

Dear Sagittarius,

I know you will be happy now that you're in your new life but there are a few things I want you to know and understand that you overlooked when we were together.

Then list all the annoying habits, ideas, proposals, plans that your (ex) Sagittarius indulged in. Top of the list might be their inability to take your ideas into account.

Make sure you write every little detail, down to the toothbrushes in the bathroom and the amount of times they said things like: "You really ought to do this, or that," or "You're looking very fat today."

Keep writing until you can write no more, then end your letter with something similar to the following:

Even though we went through hell together and never saw eye to eye I wish you well on your path.
… or some other positive comment.

Then take the letter somewhere windy and high, out of town maybe where you won't be disturbed. Maybe the top of a hill overlooking a beautiful view, on a pier during a blustery day or maybe on a cliff face, but do be sensible and don't put yourself in any personal danger.

Read through your letter again. Make sure it sounds right in your head then ceremoniously tear a small part of your letter into the smallest pieces possible and let those small pieces of paper be whisked away by the wind.

I don't think I good idea to dispose of *all* of your letter in this way, because a) it might be

rather long and you'd be guilty of littering, and b) you also run the risk of it blowing somewhere inconvenient, so save the rest of it. When you get home, burn the rest of the letter safely in an ashtray and pop it in the rubbish or put it in the paper shredder and add to your paper recycling.

Water Sign

If you are a Water sign: Cancer, Scorpio or Pisces it might be a little harder for you to recover from your broken heart. Not impossible but you might lie awake at night wondering if you've done the right thing by finishing the relationship, or feeling deeply hurt that the relationship has ended. Don't fret. Things will get better but you need to be able to get through those first difficult weeks without bursting into tears all the time.

Your emotional healing needs to encompass the Water Element. So here is a well-used suggestion.

This is a powerful way to heal the emotional hurt that has resulted since the relationship ended. It allows you to use that part of you that is most 'in tune' with the issue.

It involves your tears.

The next time you feel weepy, collect your tears into a glass. This isn't as hard as it sounds. There you are, tears falling at a rapid rate, threatening to flood the world, all you need is *one* of those tears to fall into a glass of water. I recommend using a nice glass. Something pretty, that has some meaning to you.

Ensure the tear has fallen in, then top-up with enough water almost to the rim of the glass.

Place the glass on a table, maybe with a lit candle, maybe with a photo of you together, whatever feels right for you, then recite the following:

This loving relationship with you... (Sagittarius name) has ended.

I reach out across time and space to you.

My tears will wash away the hurt I feel.

I release you from my heart, mind and soul.

We part in peace.

Then slowly drink the water.

Spend the next few weeks talking about how you feel to someone who truly cares. If there isn't anyone who can fill the role, consider a counsellor or therapist. EFT, Emotional Freedom Technique, www.emofree.com,[9] is very useful in these situations and you'll find it's easy enough to learn at home.

Your Sagittarius Friend

As I mentioned in the introduction, I have a very dear Sagittarius friend. He's actually the brother of an old school friend of mine. When we were much younger he would take me for trips on his 750cc motorbike, with me clinging to his back, hoping I wouldn't fall. I knew his family very well, as I lived with them for about a year and his mother was a lovely Leo lady. However, I later found out she was worried that he and I might fall in love... which we didn't. That was never on the cards, we were just very good friends.

He loved foreign travel too, and one of his earlier jobs was in teaching, where he met his first wife. Now he himself is half-German half-Chinese, and that wife came from a West Indian island.

The family all travelled there for the wedding, so did I; but my father had only just died, so it wasn't an entirely happy experience.

Years after his divorce he met his present wife online as she lived in the USA. The point I am making is distance for a Sagittarius is no object. They will happily travel literally to the ends of the earth for whatever they might be seeking.

So, if you have a Sagittarius friend, keep in mind that it doesn't matter a jot where you live, they will happily visit you wherever you are.

Here we have a female Pisces talking about her Sagittarius friend:

I have known my Sagittarius friend for over forty years, she is one of the best people I have ever known. A close personal friend. I have also known her in the workplace. She is loyal, trustworthy – talking to her is like a confessional. She does not suffer fools gladly but can give the impression of being a soft touch – but is quite the contrary! When I have moved around the country she is the one to send a card, make a phone call, thinks of others. She has a strong sense of duty, is close to her family, sometimes forgets self in helping others. In the workplace (her family business) she was a tough cookie – and very hardworking – she never asked staff to do what she did not do herself. Oh yes! Typical sports interest – we used to play squash and she loves racing and football.

Your Sagittarius Mum

Now keeping in mind all the things we've said about Sagittarius wanting to be free, to travel, to have a philosophical debate about 'Life, The Universe... and Everything', you'll not be surprised to know that being a mum can be a challenge for a Sagittarius. It doesn't come naturally.

Milayo is an 'amazing woman' according to her Aquarius son Nkera (who we met in *How to Bond with an Aquarius*). She was born in Nigeria and lost both her parents by her late teens. She came to England to study and work as a nurse while also supporting her two younger brothers who were left with relatives in Nigeria. She married but delayed having children so she could support her brothers. Eventually she had children and the family went back to Nigeria. In Nigeria, there was always some relative: an uncle or a cousin who came to live with them from Milayo's extended family. She started a business as a clothes shop owner. Years later, due to economic pressures, she returned to England to work again as a nurse. Her husband stayed at the house in Nigeria, which now has the next generation of Milayo's relatives living there and she still sends money to help support them.

Here Nkera describes what she is like:

*She has a big personality... .you can hear her laughing and talking loudly... no, **shouting** down the phone to her friends and then, if you were trying to watch TV, forget about it! Sometimes, I just need to escape from the noise!*

Thankfully, I don't still live with her. She can be quite impulsive and once she gets an idea, there's almost no talking her out of it (if indeed you can get a word in) and she expects everyone to come along for the ride! This can sometimes cause a problem if the idea is about something I or someone else should do, because while I'm still examining the idea, she has already got the next few steps planned out and is probably taking action like I agreed in the first place. And, as I don't do going along for the ride very well, it can cause a clash if I don't agree.

Underneath it all, though, her heart is as big as her personality and she believes she has been put on this world to help people (her family) and often fantasizes of winning the lottery and dividing up the money amongst us… but then, she just wouldn't be able to resist telling us what to do with our share! Honestly!

Notice how Nkera's biggest complaint is about her 'ideas' (a key word for Aquarius). It isn't about how she provides for the family, it's her enthusiasm for a project that sweeps everyone away when they've barely had time to digest the information.

Notice too how she quite happily has travelled hundreds of miles, across sea and land to get to another country and provide for her brood. She even still sends money home, as she feels she's been 'put on this earth' to help people.

Here is the young lady we met earlier from Baltic States in Northern Europe talking about her grandmother:

My Taurus mother often complained that my grandmother was always a workaholic and never really cared about the family. She would go to work even if her children were sick home, even if she didn't have to, she would look for excuses to get out of the house. Couldn't stay home all day. I remember my mother saying often how bad she felt when she was little and sick and with no mommy by her side… Just because she 'had' to go to work.

So to get the best from your Sagittarius mother, we need to consider first what Element you are. We discussed them in Chapter Two.

If you're an Earth sign, as in the example above, you're going to find having a Fire sign mother quite challenging. An Earth sign needs to have their physical, pragmatic, tangible needs met. So, that's Breakfast, Dinner, Lunch and Tea. Nothing else can happen until those things are organised (especially if you're a Taurus). So, if your mum, a bit like Pisces Mum, is busy following some weird new craze and is so caught up in it that you feel you're going to starve to death, or go crazy with all the excitement, then you will have to learn early in life to fend for yourself. Take cookery lessons, get someone to show you how to make food... and feed yourself. You'll feel much happier and less stressed.

If you're a Water sign, you will need time to yourself. You'll need a room you can lock yourself away in, and generally the bathroom is the suitable place so you can splash around in some water for a while.

If you're an Air sign, you will enjoy all the ideas and might even have some good old rows, and kiss and make up later. Don't expect to see eye-to-eye with everything.

If you're a Fire sign, STAND BACK! You and your Sagittarius mother are going to have lots of fun, oodles of rows, she won't back down, you won't back down... Maybe learn how to drive early, so you can get out of the house when things become too heated and assuming you haven't got clashing Moons, you should get on rather well.

Your Sagittarius Dad

I obviously can only speak from my own experience of having a Sagittarius Dad and most of the time it was fun. There were occasions when he lost his temper and we got boshed, especially if he was watching the news and we were making a noise, but overall it was a positive experience.

He especially liked taking us on holiday. As he had spent so much time travelling himself, he knew at least *something* about wherever we visited. We would have a running commentary of everything he knew about where we were going, interesting facts, local customs, favourite foods. You name it and he knew it. He was also multilingual and no matter where we went he would always manage to have some sort of conversation with, or at the very least be able to be polite to, whoever we were with. He was not shy or retiring. He was not quiet. As he drove the family car he would suddenly burst into song and sing something from a Gilbert and Sullivan operetta. He also liked the Latin Mass, as there was lots of singing with that too. And he was especially fond of his religion. He also liked deep philosophical discussions, but I never seemed old enough to be included in these and he died when I was only 22.

He loved travelling and spent most of the year on aeroplanes or in hotels. This was his true Sagittarius spirit. He liked to drive fast (Sun in the first house), adored John Wayne and kept a stack of library books, which he would read every day. If we went to the library and didn't use all our loan allocation, he would use ours so he could get as many books as possible.

He got on well with all of his family and kept in contact with them.

In this family Dad is Sagittarius and Mom is Aries:

My Dad is a Sagittarius some might say typical. The best way we know how to relate with each other these days is by cracking jokes. He loves encouraging laughter. My Mom is kind of complex, but somehow they managed to fall for each other. She may look quiet in public, but at home she's a loud mouth. They both act childish, it's like watching two little kids interact. It's cute!

He loves going out, she likes staying home. He gets a kick out of watching crazy shows like Jerry Springer, she wants to watch Martha Stewart. They are kind of opposite yet the same. He has cheated over the years too – he still has pictures of his ex-women. I think if two people are meant to be they don't need to bend for the

*other. If you are going to 'change' it should be both of you together
– for the better.*

It sounds like Mom gives as good as she gets... and that strong
Aries spirit won't let the equally strong Sagittarius spirit push
her around. Fire meets Fire!

In my family Mum is an Aquarius, so everything was all
about ideas... and my dad never stood in the way of any of her
ideas, so they both were very happy. He was quite a romantic at
times. They celebrated their 25th wedding anniversary in Vienna,
retaking their wedding vows... and he wrote poetry.

Time Waits
Still as the sense of death
Rode the night in the stars
Wrapping each shaded lamp
With a fold of eternity
But where the little bars
Of moonlight stroked the yawning hills
The shadows melted, stamped
Cold and quivering, loosing their unity.
Breezes blow soft from the North
Moaning through pines
In the valley, the lines
Of crops whisper of movement.
The plough, still aslant by a byre
Tells of fields and their ways.
Seared wood near a stricken fire
Of men and forgotten days.
Chaff from a broken shed
Wafts over the crumbling brick
Falling shyly to colour the ploughland ridges
A bed creaks and in the fields
Crops, trees and time

Wait.

Noel English

Life was never boring with my dad, there was always some sort of idea or project on the boil, or some family drama that needed attention like marrying the 'wrong religion' or 'having children out of wedlock'. He didn't do relaxation very well, or sit still for very long, there were always 'things to do'.

To get on well with your Sagittarius Dad the same advice applies as far as your Element goes, so read Sagittarius Mum for suggestions.

Your Sagittarius Sibling

To get on well with your Sagittarius sibling, keep in mind their motivating forces and learn how to get the best from your relationship.

It helps if you try and resist telling them what to do. It also helps if you rein them in if they get so worked up about something, they're prepared to sacrifice their stability for it.

My brother is a Sagittarius, and he's always at his worst when he's angry. He's always putting me down and he always wants the last word in an argument. God, he just pushes every button and he turns into a total smart Alec. I admit, he really knows how to make people look like idiots, but he's really arrogant without noticing it.

I'm not sure that making people look like idiots is a good idea but you can see here between these two brothers how there is a constant 'needing to be right'.

This young lady is an Aquarius, and she gets on very well with her Sagittarius brother:

My brother is a Sag and pretty much the only one in my family that really understands me. I see a lot of similarities with me: very laid back, slightly detached at times, we love filling our brains with new info, wacky sense of humor, and the conversations are NEVER boring. He doesn't get involved in anyone else's business and doesn't lie or talk about anyone behind their backs. He's always very straightforward but not in a mean or rude way. Doesn't take any crap from anyone either. He's just an all around cool person and even though I'm in my 20's I still look up to my brother the same way I did when I was six. Sags are cool beans indeed!

As you can see from this example, the joint Aquarius/Sagittarius need for freedom rates very highly, hence them getting on well.

Compare this to this young lady who is Gemini and her sister is Sagittarius:

Why is it that my Sagittarius sister and I always fight? They say our horoscopes are a match? Okay it's true what they say. We are the exact opposite of each other. We always hate each other and we always will. As a Gemini I'm emotional, sensitive and talkative. She is careless which is true and always doing horrific emotionally racking stuff. It's gone to the point I've almost killed myself for being so angry. So why do they say Geminis and Sagittarius are a match?

The problem here is about communication style. Gemini does love to chat. Sagittarians only want to talk about the things that are 'meaningful' (to them) and can easily become bored just chatting about less 'important' things. Gemini loves a good conversation and no one has to 'win'. They just love the pinging about that a good conversation can have. Sagittarius will have all these grand ideas about the world and won't want them challenged in any way... and Gemini loves to ask "Why"... and if they don't get an answer they can picture in their mind, they'll ask "Why" again... and if your Sagittarius isn't so good at explaining what they're on about, which can happen, they'll then feel challenged and like all Fire signs, will just go into 'attack' mode.

If you're a Water or Earth sign, unless you have compatible Moons and Ascendants, you won't get so worked up about your Sagittarius sibling, and will be more capable of steering your own course through life. You won't be so worried about all these 'ideas' floating around, and most likely will not really understand why they are the way they are. But hopefully, now you've read this far, you now will.

I hope you have enjoyed learning a little about Astrology and a little about Sagittarius the Sun sign. If you'd like more information, please visit my website www.maryenglish.com.

I am writing this while the Moon is in Sagittarius, in my office in the city of Bath, the hot-spring city in South West England. I am a Pisces. I am happy in my job, with my son, with my lovely husband and with my family .

I know that all life is made from good and bad and I decided, not so long ago, to focus on the good. There is a candle burning by me and I am imagining that the flame is burning to help you focus on the good too. If we all understood each other a little more, maybe we'd get on better. I wish you all the peace in the world... and happiness too.

References

1. *The Dawn of Astrology*, page 41, 2008, Nicholas Campion, Continuum Books, London SE1 7NX
2. *The Karmic Journey*, 1990, Judy Hall, Arkana, Penguin Group, London W8 5TZ, England
3. *Hands Across Time: The Soulmate Enigma*, 1997, Judy Hall, Findhorn Press, Forres, Scotland, IV36 0TZ
   The Astrologers and Their Creed, 1971, Christopher McIntosh, Arrow Books Ltd, 3 Fitzroy Square, London W1
4. *Becoming Jane Austen: A Life*, Jon Spence, 2003, Continuum, 11 York Road, London SE1 7NX
   Blake's Selected Poems, William Blake, 1995, Dover Publications Inc, NY 11501
5. http://www.feminist.com/resources/artspeech/interviews/janefonda.html
6. http://www.bbc.co.uk/programmes/b00zgqdl
7. http://www.telegraph.co.uk/culture/film/starsandstories/4387970/Brad-Pitt-interview-why-I-had-to-face-my-own-mortality.html
8. *Cunningham's Encyclopedia of Crystal, Gem and Metal Magic*, by Scott Cunningham
9. http://www.emofree.com

Further Information

Further Reading

An Astrological Study of the Bach Flower Remedies, by Peter Damian, 1997, published by Neville Spearman Publishers/CW Daniel Company Ltd, 1 Church Path, Saffron Walden, Essex CB10 1JP

Astrology for Dummies, 1999, IDG Books Worldwide, Inc, CA 94404

Information and Resources

The Astrological Association www.astrologicalassociation .com

The Bach Centre, The Dr Edward Bach Centre, Mount Vernon, Bakers Lane, Brightwell-cum-Sotwell, Oxon, OX10 0PZ, UK www.bachcentre.com

Ethical Dating Site www.natural-friends.com

Astrological Chart Information

Chart information and birth data from astro-databank at www.astro.com and www.astrotheme.com.

Bette Midler, 1st December 1945, Honolulu, HI, USA, 2.19pm, Aries Ascendant, Sun in 8th, Moon in Scorpio

Sammy Davis, Jr, 8th December 1925, New York, NY, USA, 1.20pm, Aries Ascendant, Sun in 9th, Moon in Virgo

Anna Freud, 3rd December 1895, Vienna, Austria, 3.15pm, Taurus Ascendant, Sun in 7th, Moon in Gemini

Christina Onassis, 11th December 1950, New York, NY, USA, 3pm, Taurus Ascendant, Sun in 7th, Moon in Capricorn

Bhagwan Shree Osho Rajneesh, 11th December 1931, Kutchwada, India, 5.13pm, Gemini Ascendant, Sun in 7th, Moon in Capricorn

Ann Souter Gloag, 10th December 1942, 3.45pm, Perth, Scotland, Gemini Ascendant, Sun in the 7th, Moon in Capricorn

Maurice Denis, 25th November 1870, Granville, France, 4pm, Gemini Ascendant, Sun in 7th, Moon in Capricorn

Paul Hewitt, 22nd November 1949, Toronto, Canada, 6.19pm, Gemini Ascendant, Sun in 6th, Moon in Capricorn

William Blake, 28th November 1757, London, UK, 7.45pm, Cancer Ascendant, Sun in 5th, Moon in Cancer

Randy Newman, 28th November 1943, Los Angeles, CA, USA, 8.02pm, Cancer Ascendant, Sun in 5th, Moon in Sagittarius

Tina Turner, 26th November 1939, Nutbush, TN, USA, 10.10pm, Leo Ascendant, Sun in 4th, Moon in Aquarius

Client X, 17th December 1953, New York, NY, USA, 8.13pm, Leo Ascendant, Sun in the 5th, Moon in Taurus

Winston Churchill, 30th November 1894, 1.30am, Woodstock, England, Virgo Ascendant, Sun in 3rd, Moon in Libra

Walt Disney, 5th December, 1901, Chicago, IL, USA, 12.35am, Virgo Ascendant, Sun in 3rd, Moon in Libra

Woody Allen, 1st December 1935, Bronx, NY, USA, 10.55pm, Virgo Ascendant, Sun in 4th, Moon in Aquarius

Jane Austen, 16th December 1775, Stevenson, UK, 11.45pm, Virgo Ascendant, Sun in 4th, Moon in Libra

Frank Sinatra, 12th December 1915, Hoboken, NJ, USA, 3am, Libra Ascendant, Sun in 2nd, Moon in Pisces

Britney Spears, 2nd December 1981, 1.30am, McComb, MS, USA, Libra Ascendant, Sun in 3rd, Moon in Aquarius

Jennifer Carpenter, 7 December 1979, Louisville, KY, USA, 3am, Libra Ascendant, Sun in 2nd, Moon in Cancer

Noel Coward, 16th December 1899, Teddington, UK, 2.30am, Libra Ascendant, Sun in 3rd, Moon in Gemini

Beethoven, 16th December 1770, Bonn, Germany, 3.40am, Scorpio Ascendant, Sun in 2nd, Moon in Sagittarius

Edith Piaf, 19th December 1915, Paris, France, 5am, Scorpio Ascendant, Sun in 2nd, Moon in Gemini

Uri Geller , 20th December 1946, Tel Aviv, Palestine, 2.30am, Scorpio Ascendant, Sun in 2nd , Moon in Scorpio

Mark Twain, 30th November 1835, Florida, MO, USA, 4.45am, Scorpio Ascendant, Sun 1st, Moon in Aries

Keith Richards, 18th December 1943, Dartford, UK, 6am, Scorpio Ascendant, Sun in 2nd, Moon in Virgo

Gary Gilmore, 4th December 1940, McCarney, TX, USA, 6.30am, Scorpio Ascendant, Sun in 1st, Moon in Aquarius

Benjamin Disraeli, 21st December 1804, London, UK, 5.30am, Scorpio Ascendant, Sun in 2nd, Moon in Leo

Brad Pitt, 18th December 1963, Shawnee, OK, USA, 6.31am, Sagittarius Ascendant, Sun in 1st, Moon in Capricorn

Jonathan Cainer, 18th December 1957, London, UK, 8am, Sagittarius Ascendant, Sun in 1st, Moon in Scorpio

Jimi Hendrix, 27th November 1942, Seattle, WA, USA, 10.15am, Sagittarius Ascendant, Sun in 12th, Moon in Cancer

Bruce Lee, 27th November 1940, San Francisco, USA, 7.07am, Sagittarius Ascendant, Sun in 12th, Moon in Scorpio

Jane Fonda, 21st December 1937, Manhattan, NY, USA, 9.14am, Capricorn Ascendant, Sun in 12th, Moon in Leo

J Paul Getty, 15th December 1892, 8.43am, Minneapolis MN, USA, Capricorn Ascendant, Sun in the 12th, Moon in Scorpio

Boris Karloff, 23rd November 1887, London, Ascendant Capricorn, Sun in 11th, Moon in Pisces

Janis Joplin, 19th January 1943, Port Arthur, TX, USA, 9.45am, Aquarius Ascendant, Sun 12th, Moon Cancer

Christina Aguilera, 18th December 1980, Staten Island, New York, USA, 10.46am, Aquarius Ascendant, Sun in 11th, Moon in Taurus

Jim Morrison, 8th December 1943, Melbourne Fl, USA, 11.55am, Aquarius Ascendant, Sun in 11th, Moon in Taurus

Kim Basinger, 8th December 1953, Athens, Georgia, USA, 11.04am, Aquarius Ascendant, Sun in 11th, Moon in Capricorn

Einaudi, 23rd November 1955, Turin, Italy, 12pm, Aquarius Ascendant, Sun in the 10th, Moon in Pisces

Robin Williamson, 24th November 1943, Glasgow, UK, 2.50pm, Pisces Ascendant, Sun in 9th, Moon in Libra

Dion Fortune, 6th December 1890, Llandudno, Wales, Moon in Libra

Gilbert O'Sullivan, 1st December 1946, Waterford, Ireland, Moon in Pisces

Index

Third House 42
Turner, Tina 31, 61
Twain, Mark 35

Z
Zeus 8
Zodiac 1, 6, 41

W
Waite, Herbert T 11
Williamson, Robin 33

Also by Mary L English
6 Easy Steps in Astrology
The Birth Charts of Indigo Children
How to Survive a Pisces (O-Books)
How to Bond with an Aquarius (O-Books)
How to Cheer Up a Capricorn (O-Books)

Please visit Mary's site at www.maryenglish.com